Business and IT: Bridging the Gap

A. A. Alchaita

KNOWLEDGE BAKERS

Cataloging in Publication Data--DK
Courtesy: D.K. Agencies (P) Ltd. <docinfo@dkagencies.com>

Alchaita, A. A., author.
Business and IT : bridging the gap / AA Alchaita.
pages cm
Includes bibliographical references and index.
ISBN 9788194498667

1. Business--Information technology. 2. Business--Data processing. I. Title.

LCC HF5548.2.A43 2020 | DDC 650.0285 23

ISBN 978-81-944986-6-7

Published by : **Knowledge Bakers**
Pune, India

Digitally Printed at : **Replika Press Pvt. Ltd.**

Preface

Over the past few years information technology (IT) and business alignment has become a great concern to organizations. To achieve alignment has become a daunting task for organizations due to rapid changes in business environment and lack of IT support. In business organizations business processes and IT are interrelated and interact with each other where one entity influences to another entity i.e. evolution in business processes requires evolution in IT and vice versa. When this co-evolution is not well aligned, a gap is created due to wrong configuration between business requirements and IT deployment.

Organizations usually strive to bridge the gap by implementing business and IT strategies (i.e. top-down planning) and tend to ignore other aspects of the co-evolution. Alignment is a continuous co-evolutionary process in which all components of business and IT are interrelated and enhance organization performance. The co-evolution between business and IT is not restricted to a level but it occurs at all levels and therefore, it is necessary to understand and study co-evolution at all levels within organizations. This book presents a co-evolutionary framework that helps to study and understand the co-evolution at three levels i.e. strategic level, operational level and individual level in an integrated fashion. The three levels need to co-evolve so that all components at each level co-evolve. This framework will speed up the alignment in organizations. We argue that the lack of knowledge of business among IT people and IT knowledge among business executives may cause the gap; therefore, a need arises to have a knowledgeable mediator between the domains that could help in the co-evolution. A K-mediator (i.e. knowledge mediator) has been used in the proposed co-evolutionary framework that facilitates the co-evolution at each level.

I hope this book is widely read. If we are to avoid the blunders of the past, then we need to change the direction and start benefiting from the knowledge base created by the writers. We did not have this chance a decade ago. Now is the right time. There are many people I need to thank for their help and support in writing this book.

Considerable thanks go to my professor and his team. Needless to say I thank my mother, father and siblings for their encouragement, love and support on my long road.

A A Alchaita

Contents

1

Introduction

This chapter provides a description of the background and rationale for carrying out the research and describes different issues and problems that need to be addressed. It also provides a description of the research purpose, the questions being addressed in the research and the significance of the study.

1.1 Motivation and Rationale to Conducting Research

Information technology (IT) now is an essential part of business organizations and, therefore, a greater interdependence between IT and business has evolved. As digital computing has evolved during the last 35 years, the IT industry has grown and provided a number of tools for business growth and new models in order to support business processes and make them more efficient. Business organizations throughout the world are investing millions of dollars and pounds in order to acquire IT solutions for their business processes. Likewise, IT companies are spending enormous amounts in research and development in order to meet business requirements. Information technology in general has penetrated into business operation worldwide and businesses have become more dependent on IT and its products and services. Predominantly, a change in local and global marketplace forces business organizations to adopt IT and its services in order to be competitive in the marketplace, otherwise they may lose customers and business. The high dependency of business organizations on IT and its products places high demand on IT organizations to develop and deliver effective, efficient and high quality applications in order to meet business requirements in a timely manner. Evolution of businesses and their requirements constantly put pressure on IT and its products in order to be of high quality. ,...All precepts such as 'reusing software', 'reengineering the business', 'domain engineering', and 'component based development' become mere slogans if the necessary software does not properly meet business needs[1]". The growing business requirements create opportunities for new technologies, and advancements in technology provide new business processes and models. Therefore, business processes and IT co-evolve and in turn co- evolutionary changes generate successes in business organizations.

When organizations adopted IT and started using it at large scale throughout the business, the organizational structures are also modified.

Organizations have realized the importance of a centralized IT department which will be responsible for the development and maintenance of technologies. Albeit, new organizational structure improved the efficiency in operating business by using IT, it also created a gap of communication between business executives and IT department. This business-IT gap is created due to the misalignment between business requirements and supporting IT.

Researchers and practitioners recognize the importance of business-IT alignment. Although, the alignment is important but difficult to achieve, organizations strive to develop an effective process for alignment so that it can not only fulfill the technical needs but also accomplish the business objectives too. Many researchers have developed models and used different survey instruments in order to measure alignment between business and IT [77][123][124][125].

Businesses always face challenges such as marketplace, competitors, political situation and legislation that cause change in requirements. Large businesses such as financial institutions, the auto industry and telecommunication that have various products and services are forced to alter their business requirements due to above stated factors. The continuous development in IT brings up the need to adapt existing and old system in order to provide more reliable, efficient and effective business processing.

IT-service businesses recognize the gap between the two entities. Business people consider strategy, problems and external pressure, while IT personnel think about platform, middleware, network and applications. In business communication an informal and natural languages is used whereas IT requires a formal and artificial language in a specific background for task processing. Due to the co-evolution between business and IT there will always be a gap between the two entities and increasingly the need to bridge the gap is a paramount concern in organizations.

There is a need of a framework that could facilitate organizations to understand co-evolution in an integrated way. A co-evolutionary approach helps to understand the reasons for the gap. This approach suggests a framework that could assist organizations for reducing the gap and estimate the rate of evolution of business and technology.

1.2 The Gap between Business and Information Technology

It is well known that IT services and products directly affect business processes and play an essential role in organization success. Adoption of IT in businesses has shown significant increase in efficiency that achieved higher return on sales than those businesses without or low IT efficiency [2]. But simply adding IT to existing business processes will never provide the desired and competitive advantages. For a better support through IT services and products it is important to redesign business processes. Co-evolution in both business requirements and

IT at the same time has great impact on businesses but this rarely happens as the rate of evolution between both business processes and IT is different. With the advancements in business processes usually IT remains intact or vice versa and hence a misalignment occurs. Figure 1.1 shows a simple misalignment model between business and IT where business processes are evolved (i.e. addition of new service in black circle) but the supporting technologies do not evolve and therefore, a misalignment occurs [128]. This misalignment may be due to the financial constraints that do not allow deploying new technologies to support the new business process.

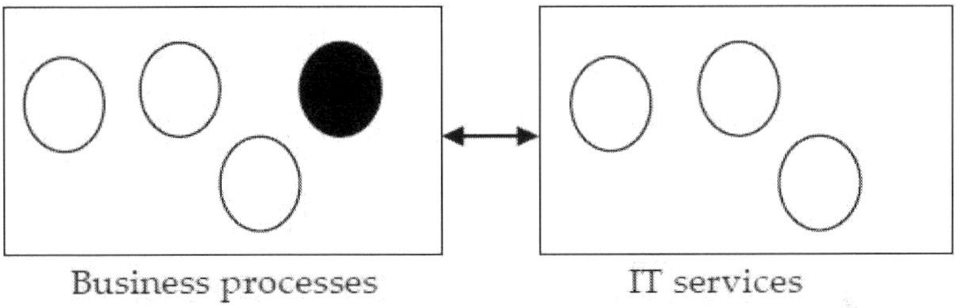

Figure 1.1 A misalignment model

A change in business processes affects IT and requires new system that could fulfill the new business requirements. Since financial constraints do not allow technology to be replaced or updated, applications are built on old technology or required functionality is added into the existing system which contributes problems in the systems.

An alignment is defined as a process of relating two systems or entities. An effective alignment greatly influences IT effectiveness and leads to superior business performance. When an entity evolves without referencing a change into another entity the alignment is disturbed. This misalignment greatly impacts on the system that depends on both the entities. A telecommunication company recently announced a process of procurement online for its employees in order to purchase items online to save time and improve employees' efficiency, but the system could not be available due to lack of supporting technologies and networking connection with the suppliers. This misalignment between business process and IT induced frustration among employees that eventually affected on their performance and business as whole. Another company introduced utility bill payment service online in order to facilitate customers, but the low bandwidth and inconvenient application interface refrained customers to use such facility. This misalignment between business and IT caused loss in business as the customers switched to another company for better, convenient and quick service. In organizations when business needs are fulfilled by applying IT in a timely and collaborative manner to achieve the organization's goals and objectives effectively, it is said there is alignment between both business and IT.

Alignment is measureable and organizations measure alignment. The importance of alignment between business and IT has been recognized a long time ago [3][4]. IT delivers systems and services that are significant to organization's strategies, operations and user requirements which can happen only in the presence of alignment. Alignment is a result of interaction between business and IT. The IT is the main entity that works with business in order to automate the processes.

The rapidly changing business requirements demand to develop new business processes and evolve the supporting IT in order to be competitive in market [5]. When business processes and supporting technologies are evolved, essentially the alignment gap should be kept a minimum between both the domains. When the gap between business and IT is minimum, then alignment is said to effective and, therefore, it improves the performance of the business. Alignment between business and IT causes more benefits including corporate agility and efficient decision making. In organizations the alignment between business and information technology is disturbed due to the miscommunication and absence of a language that is common to both the domains. In viewing this business objectives are not supported by the IT strategy and the relationship between both the entities becomes a failure. Therefore, it is necessary to have a tight alignment so that business and IT domains co-evolve effectively. Only effective collaborative partnership at all levels and continuous adjustment can sustain the alignment. A change or modification in any of the business processes and supporting technology can cause misalignment between the business and IT. The change in a process of either entity (business or IT) influences other dependent processes regardless of which process or object was modified.

1.3 Purpose of Research

The main purpose and contribution of this research is to develop an advanced understanding on the subject of co-evolution of business and information technology and to develop a framework for reduce the gap between the two entities.

The research seeks to achieve the main goal by meeting the following objectives:

- To develop a computational model for co-evolution between business and information technology
- To study and analyze the inter-relationship between business and information technology
- To develop a framework for co-evolution in order to understand co-evolution in an integrated fashion
- To evaluate the framework on financial domain

Our research focuses on the organization environment relationship as co-evolution takes place at multi levels. We hope that our framework will help to study co-evolution at three levels i.e. strategic level, operational level and individual level in an integrated fashion. As Preston *et. al.,*[83] said there is a lack of communication among business executives and IT personnel and therefore, they are unable to comprehend requirements from each other. Our framework will reduce such lacking since K-mediator tool is knowledgeable in both the domains and will assist co-evolution at each level.

Business organizations are running their businesses successfully and still survive in marketplace without using our co-evolutionary framework. They even continue to do so in future, but in fact they are not generating the revenue as they can do. Most of the organizations focus on adapting strategies at higher level in order to achieve co-evolution, but still cannot get the desired results. Our co-evolutionary framework will help organizations to co-evolve at all levels and generate higher revenue while staying within the constraints of their changing requirements. The framework is evaluated in financial domain using a case study that determined the co-evolution at each level within the organization.

1.4 Research Question

This research poses a fundamental question:

Is there any systematic and scientific theory for co-evolution that may assist in discovering a novel/efficient technique to reducing the gap between business and information technology?

This question leads to further sub-questions as:

a. *Does an integrated environment in organizations impact on the gap between business and IT ?*

b. *Is the linkage between business and information technology effective?*

The answers of the above stated two sub-questions lay the foundation for achieving overall research goal.

1.5 Organization of Book

In this book we begin with the chapter that illustrates the background of co-evolution of business and information technology and the research question of the study. Chapter 2 presents a literature review and discusses several computational models and introduces a definition of computational model. Also, it discusses evolution and co-evolution of business and information technology. The chapter also reviews related work in detail. The Chapter 3 describes the research methodology, proposed approach and relevant information. Chapter 4 discusses the business process evolution and importance of externalization of business processes, the role of IT in business processes and co-evolution between business and IT. The chapter presents a co-evolution model and discusses the co- evolutionary requirements. Chapter 5 describes the business and technology architectures and discusses several alignment frameworks. In this book we have used the terms model, framework and architecture interchangeably. The chapter also presents the importance of strategic alignment between business and IT. Finally, the chapter presents our proposed co-evolutionary framework. The Chapter 6 provides an evaluation of the architecture in the financial domain. Chapter 7 concludes the study and describes the future work.

2

Literature Review

This chapter provides review of some computational models that aid to construct foundation of the proposed co-evolutionary framework and its components. The computational models may be used to develop the proposed co-evolutionary framework in different environments. The chapter also describes an overview of evolution and co-evolution of business and IT that are fundamentals of the proposed co-evolutionary framework. In this chapter various alignment models have been reviewed that relate to the research study and some useful frameworks have been identified that may help in developing the proposed co-evolutionary framework.

2.1 A Review of Computational Models

A model is an illustration of a system that abstracts clear and certain features without showing details [129]. A model is a convenient way to analyze a complex entity by focusing on specific aspects, removing the details that are not relevant in order to see clearly one characteristics of interest. A complex technical environment like an architecture solution or business that is difficult to understand can be understood by models. A model can be developed by using other models changed from one layer to another layer of abstraction.

A computational model is a blueprint of a computation performing over particular architecture. The software industry in its all diversity aims at writing programs that can be executed efficiently in a diverse world of hardware.

2.1.1 Distributed Parallel Programming Model

A distributed computing model is composed of different computers that interact with each other for achieving a common goal [6]. The model allows distributed processing data and objects over the network of systems that are connected with each other [9]. This helpful to solve a complicated problem that requires significant time.

Evolutionary algorithms (EAs) are usually used to solve difficult and time consuming problems, therefore parallel distributed environment is useful to run

EAs and this approach has been developed successfully [7]. The evolutionary algorithms may be useful in understanding co-evolutionary study and for development of systems.

2.1.2 Client-Server Computing Model

The scalability and complexity of software applications have exposed various shortcomings in traditional computational models. It is supposed that the computers connected to a server give a best performance in terms of price and this has developed an interest in client-server model. Client-server model makes sympathetic effective computing controllable by supporting chunks of applications that are shared by different users [11]. Developers for a client-server model divide the load for processing in two different logical processes i.e. client and server. As a common model resources are distributed and in a client-server system processes for client and server can be run on different computers.

Middleware binds clients and servers together to form a unified system in a distributed client-server system. The middleware is a software layer that provides convenience of accessibility of information between clients and servers.

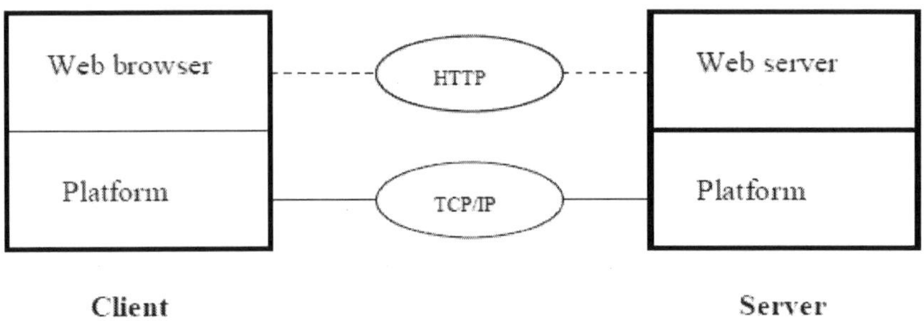

Figure 2.1: A client-server model

The figure 2.1 shows a client-server model where a client sends a request through a web browser to a server. Both client and server are connected by protocols. Upon receiving a request from a user the server sends the required data.

There are two models in a client-server architecture i.e. thin-client and fat-server model and fat-client and thin-server model. In the first type of model (i.e. the thin-client and fat-server model), the client computer manages the presentation while the major part of the functionality is carried out on the server. The functions that are implemented included in both client side and server-side. Another type of client-server model is completely different than of the first type i.e. the server in this model manages the database while the rest of the functionality is implemented by the client [12].

A very well known model in client-server field is the three-tier client server model that consists of an interface tier, a business tier and a database tier [13]. The three-tier client-server model has database server as local to the application server. Essentially for a distributed three-tier client server model, the server needs to be installed on a separate independent machine on the network. This model facilitates server application to access different databases and web services application is an example of this model. Nowadays mobile services are available and clients access the services on the move. A client-server style of communication can be used in mobile systems [10].

2.1.3 Peer-to-Peer (P2P) Computing Model

Peer-to-Peer (P2P) is a computing model that is described as a collection of distributed processing units called peers [14]. In this model several network devices or peers share resources, exchange data, communicate and collaborate in real time with each other independently without using central servers. On a P2P network a peer may interact with other peers in a multifarious fashion, for example, a complicated computational problem can be broken into different subtasks in order to run in tandem on the network to complete a given task.

Figure 2.2 shows a peer-to-peer model where different members of an organization who have been given task are working on sub-tasks in parallel. The peers share resources and exchange data in real time. Some other examples include Skype, Bittorrent, and internet telephony network where peers share and exchange data.

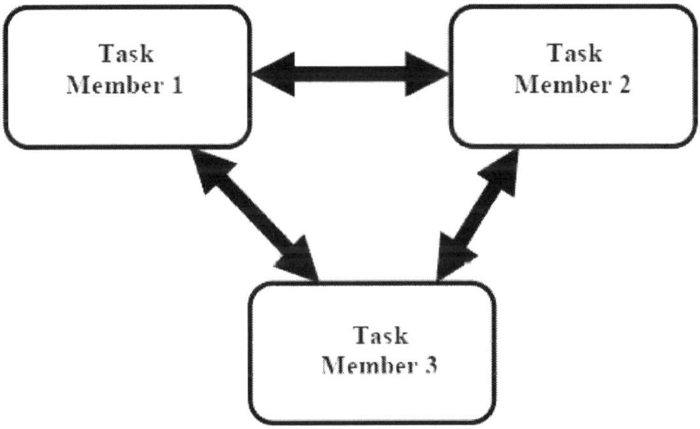

Figure 2.2: A peer-to-peer model

There are various benefits of P2P model that offers to its users and many conglomerates. One of the great benefits of P2P model is to utilize the resources that are never used such as processing power for large-scale computations and huge storage potential. Due to P2P model the restriction of single-source access has been removed. The P2P model can be used for distributing data and control. There has been a risk of single-point failure for performance optimization, but

P2P has helped in eliminating such risk. Using P2P infrastructure, organizations may save revenue by providing distributed services to the clients and replacing the data centers that involve heavy cost. Also for data backup and retrieval the storage can also be replaced toward clients. The P2P mechanism make is feasible for remote maintenance and direct access.

The bandwidth of communication is improving day by day and the continuous improvements facilitate the transfer of a large amount of data from one place to another. In a P2P environment powerful computers are required to handle services provided by the P2P infrastructure. These computers are efficient and robust so that they can have a large storage capacity and powerful processing [15].

2.1.4 Component-Based Development (CBD) Model

For a distributed computing a standard-based application/resource sharing architecture is emerged that is used to share computer and storage resources in heterogeneous systems and applications [8]. It facilitates scientists and engineers to solve large scale computing problems. This new paradigm is known as grid computing and a study of grid evolution [16] proposes that it is an integration of software migration with hardware. This study proposed a computational model in which an object has been used as a unit of computation perceived by object oriented paradigm [16]. The objects collaborate and communicate with each other.

Object and Component

An object is some piece of compiled code that provides some service to the rest of the software. An object is comprised of data and processes where data is processed by the processes. The dependency of data and processes in an object improves cohesion. Object principles have been extended by the components that explicate specification of an object with an illustration of dependency of specification called an interface. A component interface is a set of behaviors that a component object offers to its clients. At this point the client of an object and competencies of the object are at the level of indirection. These objects are called as components where computation is carried out and control started. Later the control is passed through interaction to other components [17].

Software Component

A software component has been defined in various ways and according to Kung-Kiu *et. al.,*[18] a software component is a software unit that consists of *provided services* and *required services*. The component performs provided services (i.e. operations) that are based on the required services. Another definition of a component that is based on a component model is given by Heineman *et. al.,* [19] that states component as a software element that fits to a component model. It can be deployed and composed without modification according to a composition standard.

A software component model is defined in terms of syntax, semantics and composition of components and component models can be classified according to their syntax, semantics and composition. Taxonomies of component models such as JavaBeans, Enterprise JavaBeans (EJB), Component Object Model (COM), Architecture Description Language (ADL) and Service Oriented Framework Architecture (SOFA) have been provided by [20].

In component-based software development [16] composition is the main concern. Traditionally, components perform computation and initiate control flow that make compositional reasoning less tractable. A component model [17] has been developed for separation of control flow from computation. In this model, component composition operators called exogenous connectors for component composition have been introduced that capture only control flow leaving components to encapsulate computation only. The model separates control flow from computation and hence components are independent and useful for reusability in different architectures. Figure 2.3 shows component- based development model.

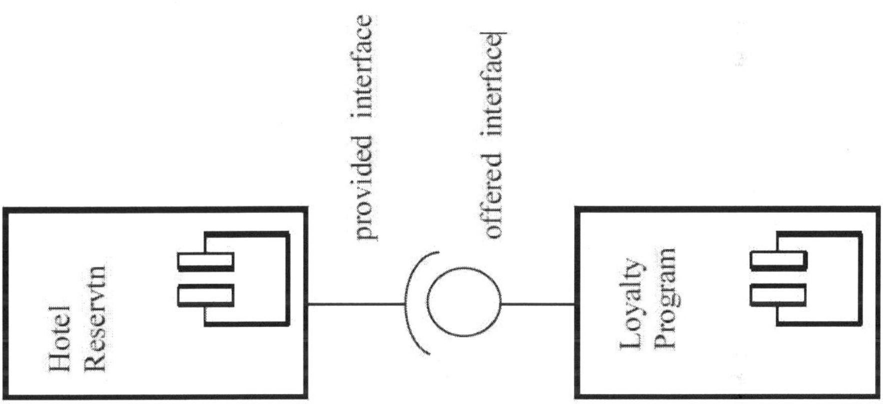

Figure 2.3: A component-based development model

2.1.5 Initial Definition of Computational Model

In order to understand the processes in the real world a model is created and based on simulation of the processes outcome of the processes is predicted. The prediction of the processes is based on the parameters that are provided as input. A computational model can be defined as:

A computational model is a set of computational codes, executable in some software/ hardware environment, that transform a set of input data into a set of output data, with the input, output, and transformation typically having some interpretation in terms of real-world phenomena. In other words a computational model is:

A model that shows how the behavior of the system is the result of the behavior of each of its components.

2.2 A Review of Evolution and Co-Evolution of Business and Information Technology

2.2.1 Evolution of Business and Information Technology

In recent years organizations have become more assiduous to provide quality products and services to their customers and, therefore, business processes in enterprises evolve over a period of time in response to demands. Business processes and rules are changed in compliance with the customers' demands and hence business evolution happens. Business processes evolve as result of new requirements or revisions on existing ones to meet the business objectives and goals. The supporting software to the business processes also evolves to using new technologies. Change in world monetary system, mergers of competitors and governmental efforts towards accelerated economic progress are creating challenges for multinational organizations, and hence, these shifts lead to business evolution which subsequently affects the underpinning technologies.

As a result of business evolution there are some reactivity issues to information technology systems. The reason for this is the lack of traceability between business and information technology systems. This lack of traceability causes a delay in adapting information technology applications to changes. This gap causes a direct impact on business analysts who cannot formalize business processes using suitable business models. This gap affects negatively on business evolution and consequently evolution rules become difficult to be used in use cases.

2.2.2 Business Process Artifacts

In business evolution various types of artifacts that constitute business processes are changed. A business process is a dynamic but complex collection of artifacts. When we analyze the definition of a process we should be able to recognize different artifacts (i.e. product, service, information, customer) those that reflect who has responsibilities and to do what business activities in the business and why the activities are performed. An easy evolution of business means that it should be easy to modify each and every artifact without causing any negative effects anywhere in the system. Since all artifacts are interconnected, therefore, evolution of business is the management of evolution of all the artifacts and the relationships between them as a system.

A framework business process management (BPM) system [21] has been developed in which a complete overview of different artifacts has been given and to make the artifacts more effective and efficient various recommendations have been suggested. In business requirements increasing changes are constantly forcing enterprises to evolve their business processes [22][23].

2.3 BUSINESS PROCESS EVOLUTION

2.3.1 Business Process

A business process consists of a specific set of coordinated tasks or activities that are related to each other in a specific way to achieve a pre-defined goal or outcome of an organization [52]. In other ways a process is a set of logically and partially ordered steps that are intended to reach a goal [52]. Hammer and Champy [53] state 'A business process is a collection of activities that takes one or more kinds of inputs and creates an output that is of value to customers. A business process has a goal and is affected by events occurring in external world or in other processes.

A business process is considered as a large as completing an entire order (from taking order to shipping and delivering order) or it can be small as just receiving an order from a customer. Figure 2.4 depicts a flow of business process

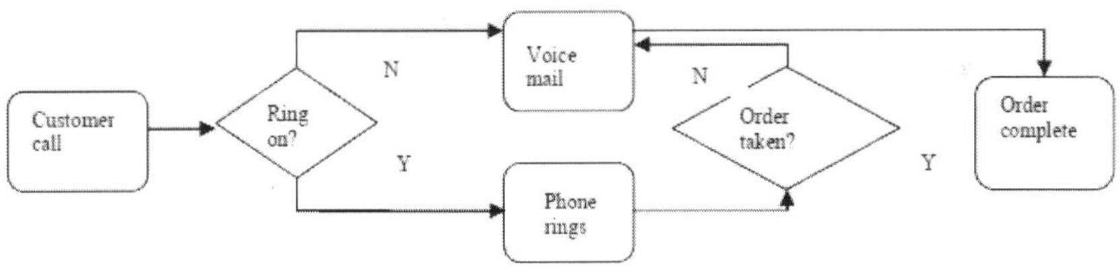

Figure 2.4 Business Process Flow

The figure 2.5 shows that a customer calls to a company to place an order where due to heavy load of calls either the order is taken by the attendant or recorded in voice mail. Businesses are increasingly becoming competitive and changing rapidly in order to reducing the operational cost while maintaining high quality standards of the products and services. It is important to understand and manage business processes effectively and, therefore, researchers have paid much attention and put effort towards understanding business processes.

2.3.2 Business Process Management

Organizations can perform better and become more efficient by changing their business processes. Organizations need business processes that could enable business strategy to be implemented and to achieve business aims and objectives [136]. In today's business environment flexible and adaptable applications are required in order to meet the desired changes in business rules and policies. Enterprises can improve their business efficiency by using Business Process Management (BPM) tools. A business process management tool is a systematic approach that helps business processes to become more capable and efficient of adapting changes in business environment. A business process management consists of methods and techniques to support analysis, design and administration of business processes [54]. To complete a business process essentially all the tiny business steps must be understood as they are required in analysis and design of BPM flows [59]. Most organizations have their own business process management system (i.e. collection of business processes).

Businesses rely on the processes and services that are offered to their customers. Information technology supports the services to improving business efficiency and hence the notion of Service Oriented Architecture (SOA) has emerged. A business is a coherent set of processes that are controlled by business people and constitute a management model while IT people consider business as a set of IT services that constitute implementation and are controlled by IT people. In a business process management system the processes and services are not distinctive and, therefore, difficult to be evolved individually.

Since a BPM system is comprised of different artifacts such as processes, technology, organizational structure, policies and stakeholders, it is imperative to know that a desire in developing BPM system may affect these artifacts as well.

As all artifacts are interconnected and interdependent, it is necessary to develop a model of business processes so that each artifact is more productive and efficient.

2.3.3 Business Process Modeling

A business model consists of different components that include corporate structure, revenues, operating strategies, processes, target audience, product and services [53]. A business model has been categorized by Scott *et. al.,* [55] and developed an affinity diagram [56] showing different components of a business model. The figure 2.5 depicts organizations create values in marketplace by the resources/asset they have by using the resources through business processes or activities. Strategically they can choose among customers, competitors, revenue or strategy to develop businesses and their value network can be enhanced by establishing a customer relationship and product line. The financial aspects and profit help capturing the value in marketplace.

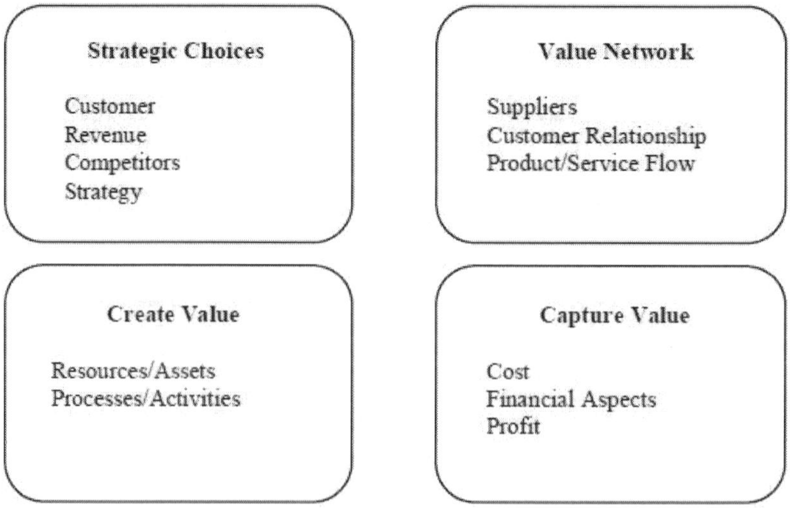

Figure 2.5 Business Model Affinity Diagram

Business process modeling has become a necessity for enterprises in order to automate their business processes for better performance and efficiency. Therefore, flexibility is an inevitable principle in the designing of business processes so that customer requirements could be fulfilled by adapting business processes.

Business process modeling used a workflow approach but it was well criticized due to paucity of flexibility and its rigid description in customizing business requirements [56].

Business services are existing semantic components that have flexibility to accommodate corporate needs and they also bundle the business process fragments within them. A business service is a fragment of business process [57] and a reusable unit that has one or several process fragments for solving a business problem. A business service has three parts that show business knowledge at different levels. Figure 2.6 depicts a business service

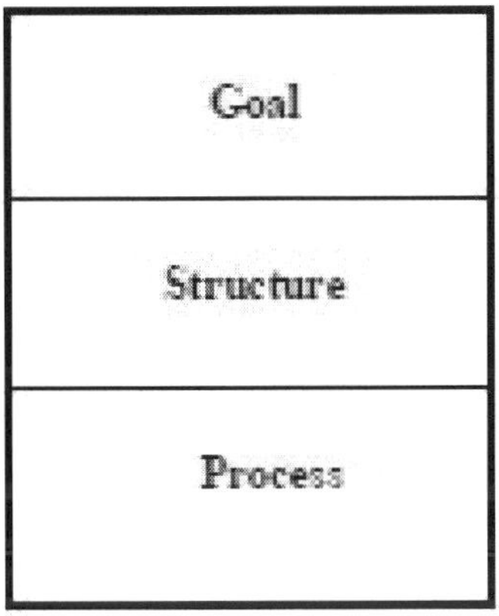

Figure 2.6 A Business Service

In the figure 2.6 the Goal part states the purpose of the service i.e. the problem to be solved by the service, the Structure part is about the process organization for achieving the goal, and Process is the solution offered by the service.

2.3.4 Business Process Evolution

Enterprises are innovating their business processes and supporting IT services in order to meet the swift changes in business requirements [23][53]. As we stated earlier that in a business process management all artifacts are interrelated and interdependent, therefore, a successful evolution of a business process depends on evolution of each artifact. It is important for a business evolution that all the artifacts are available in electronic form as some of them may be on paper such as rules, policies and processes. Each artifact should also be available independently and separately with its life cycle in order to work effectively.

2.3.4.1 Externalization of Business Processes

In order to evolve independently a business process should be externalized. This externalization helps the managing of dynamic reconfiguration and adaptation of application flow. We consider an example of a purchase order process to illustrate the significance of externalization in business evolution.

Consider a customer intends to purchase an item and would like to view the status of the order such as delivery schedule. The purchasing order is a complex task that requires validation, discount, business artifacts, external partners etc. The purchase order process may have sub-processes and all these services share the same data. Figure 2.7 shows the scenario

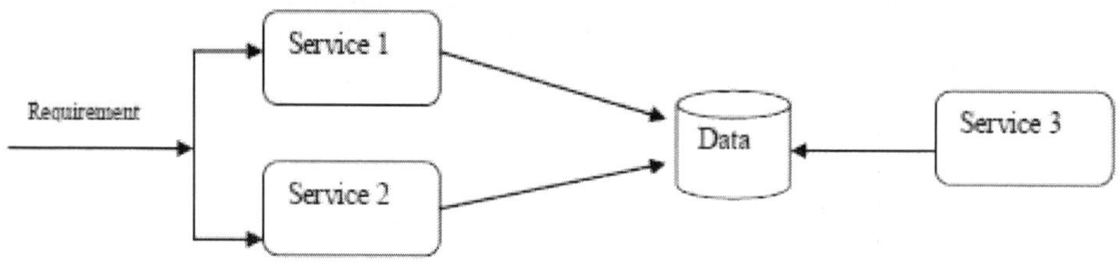

Figure 2.7 Services access same data

Since the control flows and sequences are hardcoded in the services, it is difficult to make any change, in case the business has new rules in place. Consequently the business process may not evolve effectively and efficiently. Now to make business evolution efficient, we consider the services as elements in which control flow of service operations reside. These elements access data separately and do not share any data. Figure 2.8 shows this model.

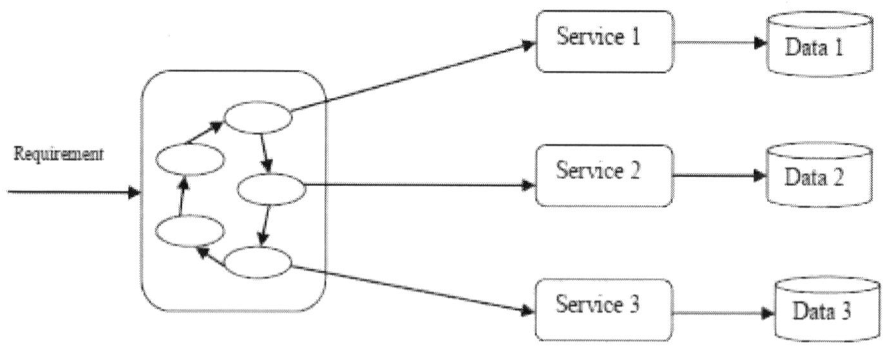

Figure 2.8 Flexible process evolution

The business process and its services are independent and its easier to make any change rather changing the entire application.

It is important to build up an understanding among all stakeholders who will be affected by a change in a business process. A change in organizations can take place in two forms i.e. incremental or continuous change and transformational or discontinuous change [57]. Continuous changes require small adjustments that are driven by internal factors such as introduction of new product or process, introduction of new technology or organizational restructure. Discontinuous changes bring major change in business and that are driven by external factors such as customers' demands, legal, political or technological change. The use of IT resources may be effective when there is a balance between internal and external resources [58]. In other words, organizations can get the benefit of IT resources when customers' demands are fulfilled by introducing new products and services online. Similarly, organizational structure is changed to provide better and expedite services to stakeholders.

2.3.4.2 Role of IT in Business Evolution

Initially the IT role was to automate business processes in order to improve their efficiency and effectiveness but with the development of technology, IT has become a significance means of gaining competitive advantage in marketplace. Senior management of organizations would always like to ask questions such as:

a) What is the significant role of IT in their business, and is the role of IT in business is fundamentally different from the role a decade before?

b) Does IT play an effective role in shaping business strategies or is IT just to support business processes?

c) What is the source of IT capability within or outside of the organizations, either by any joint venture or collaboration with another organization?

The IT role has evolved from its initial objective of supporting and automating business processes to an enabler for creating a business network of inter-organizational arrangements. Deployment of IT cannot produce the desired results if the organizational structure and culture remains intact. In other words it is important that the business processes are evolved throughout all the levels in organization in order to get maximum benefits of IT deployment. Therefore, it is necessary to identify the level where the IT benefits are in line with the efforts of the required changes in business organization. Over the time, other levels can also be explored depending on the nature of requirements, value and competitiveness in marketplace. Figure 2.9 shows different evolutionary levels with the degree of evolution and the corresponding benefits i.e. as the business evolution occurs in result of increasing evolutionary levels benefits go high until the network design (revolutionary levels) where business evolution is maximum high and so are the benefits.

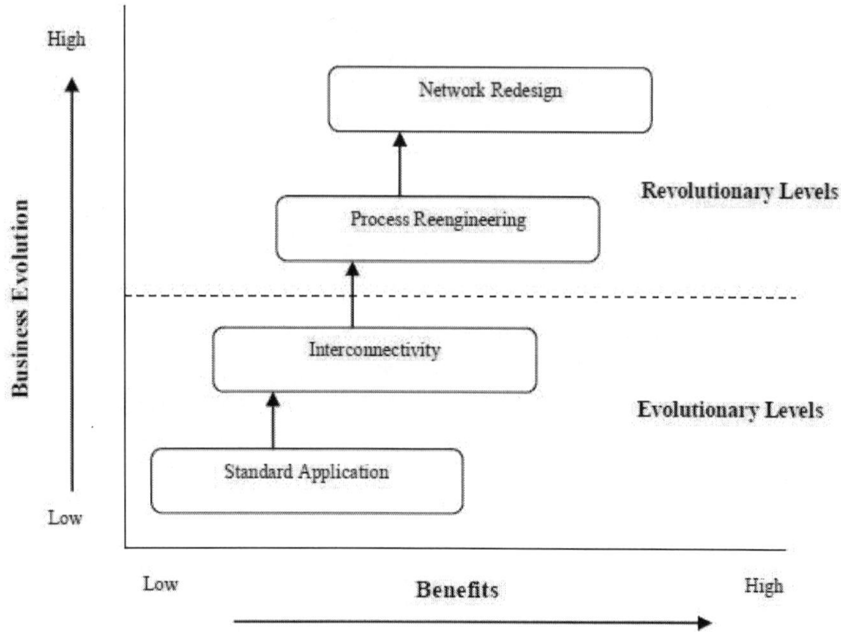

Figure 2.9 Business Evolutionary Levels

Evolutionary Levels

Evolutionary levels are defined as the levels where changes are small and incremental that do not change the whole process or bring new approach. In a business they consist of two levels i.e. primary and secondary levels. At primary level, standard applications are deployed in order to automate the business processes with minimum changes. We consider benefits from an IT application enhanced provided the performance criteria are realigned with the technology- oriented business process. The secondary level in the evolutionary level is the integration of systems, applications and business process interdependence where technical interconnectivity and challenges business process interdependence are observed. Business processes are evolved to an extent at evolutionary level where organizations obtain a range of benefits in result of that evolution.

Revolutionary Levels

The revolutionary levels are the levels where the processes are completely changed, new ideas are introduced and new approach is taken. These levels consist of process reengineering and network redesign.

In early-to-mid 1990s organization-wide transformational change was advocated under the label business process re-engineering (BPR) [53]. In order to achieve a dramatic improvement in business performance a BPR is essential process that is used to rethink and completely redesign the business processes. Business processes are changed for the betterment of current processes and are critical for the deployment of IT systems. The next level in revolutionary levels is network redesign that helps connecting external businesses such as suppliers, distributers and other intermediaries. In network redesign major functionalities such as transaction processing and inventory interchange are developed in terms of administrative and operational efficiencies [60].

IT has introduced new practices that would have been impossible without technologies. If IT infrastructure is insufficient or poor then changes in business processes may not be effective and limit the success. Therefore, IT deployment in organizations requires comprehensive changes in business processes in order to obtain maximum outcome.

The services of IT that support to business processes vary from one process to another depending on the value of the process within business organization. Figure 2.10 shows different business processes and their respective IT services i.e. process 1 has three IT services and process 5 has one IT service etc.

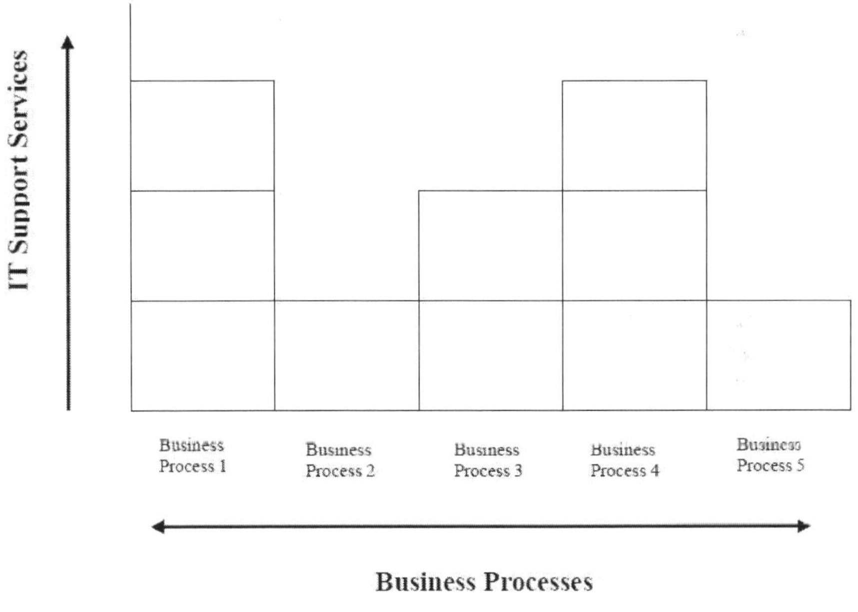

Figure 2.10 IT Support to business processes

2.4 Information Technology in Business Processes

2.4.1 The Evolving Role of IT in Business Processes

IT is evolving rapidly and is considered as knowledge of using tools and devices to perform tasks in efficient and effective manners. Historically, technology has been evolving since the Stone Age where tools made of stones, bronze- Bronze Age, and iron – Iron Age. In some specific periods many innovations grown in result of technology evolution that produced what is known as industrial revolution. Inventions such as telephone, computer, internet and wireless devices have transformed society. IT has great impact on businesses, its users and working environment. IT, which is a convergence of computing, databases, networking and imaging technologies has had a profound impact on businesses. In today's world, IT gathers data, processes, and stores to expedite communication in everyday's routine work. In few years back, IT was considered as a supporting tool in overall business plans and strategies. But now IT has become an integral part of today's businesses that is creating new opportunities for businesses, services, products and procedures. When a technology is introduced in a business organization it leads to further technological requirements in order to develop products and services.

If we consider the evolving role of computer technologies, we begin with the office automation technologies such as word-processing programs that were developed to facilitate routine office work. The dot-matrix printers and simple word-processors led to databases and networking resources supported by telecommunication and multimedia technologies [61]. The change in business processes in result of adoption of technology continued to organization transformation.

Organizations used different information systems such as Transaction Processing Systems (TPS), Management Information Systems (MIS), and Decision Support Systems (DSS) that supplemented communication technologies such as email and videotext. Imaging technologies such as barcode systems also transformed business processes that are used in superstores, libraries, security departments etc in order to speed-up processes. Technologies evolve in result of consumers and corporate demands in order to introduce and develop new products and services.

Companies are adopting IT more rapidly than before in order to be competitive in the marketplace. Internet technologies have enabled companies to expand their businesses throughout the world in order to promote products and gain maximum market share.

2.4.2 Impact of IT in Business Processes

IT plays a vital role in transformation of an organization [62] that results in economic benefits. The rapid development in telecommunication has reduced the human resources as channels of information [63] and organizations are distributing their business processes as opposed to centralization. Online databases and networking facilitate businesses to disseminate and distribute information in standard formats.

IT has greatly influenced the development and maintenance of customer relationships. IT fulfils customers' demands immediately by providing one product information and services offered. Product information and specifications or information about services offered are provided over the internet which is efficient and convenient to customers [63].

2.5 Co-Evolution of Business and Information Technology

Co-evolution is taken to mean that the evolution of one domain is partially dependent on the evolution of the other [24]. The co-evolution term and concept has been used in various disciplines. In **medicine**, the development of neuroprosthesis has changed the scope of how humans interact with the tools. The co-evolution between humans and machine have potential for restoring communication and control in disabled individuals [131]. In **engineering,** the co- evolution term has been used as animals in nature co-evolve in both form and function; this drew researchers their concern on co-evolution of both morphology and controller in robotics [132]. In **economics,** the co-evolution has been used to carry out study by Eharles *et. al.,* [133] that states cultural processes can reshape the selective pressures facing individuals and so favor the evolution of behavioural traits not previously advantaged. In **biology,** Rafael *et. al.,* [135] has conducted a study that the impact of environmental changes on co- evolutionary dynamics between host and parasites and showed by a mathematical model that when environmental factors influence the specificity of host and parasites interactions can profound effects on the co-evolutionary dynamics.

The ever growing technologies facilitate businesses to develop new models or update the existing models while the evolution in business requirements compels IT to be evolved to fulfill the business needs.

According to Wardboys *et. al.,* [25] co-evolution describes the symbiotic relationship between dynamically changing commercial environments and the software that support them. Since it is difficult for software to adapt to continuous changes in business rules, business becomes less efficient and the perceived value of software decreases. On the other hand, for an effective and efficient business the use of the latest technology is essential. Therefore, co-evolution is defined as a link/relationship between business and IT: when business requirements are changed the supporting software has also to be evolved. IT is continuously developing and new technologies are emerging. New technologies provide new business opportunities for example, eBay and Amzon.com have gained a lot benefit of new technologies to developing their business processes. Figure 2.11 depicts a co-evolution model where business processes (b1, b2, b3) are being supported by IT services (t1, t2, t3) respectively. Then after an evolution in business processes a new process b4 is added and to support the new business process evolution in IT takes place i.e. a new IT service t4 is added. Similarly, a business process b2 has evolved to b2′ and to support the process the related technology has also been updated i.e. t2′. This co-evolution clearly depicted in the figure 2.11 and is a perfect co-evolution where all the business processes have the underlying IT services.

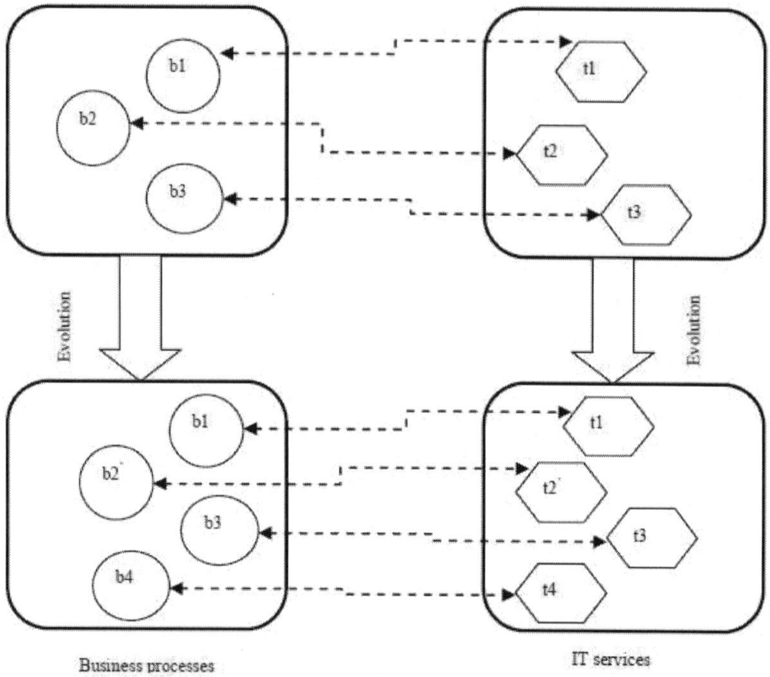

Figure 2.11 Business – IT Co-evolution

When business requirements are not supported by the IT then a gap is created in absence of such co-evolution. A changing business environment causes a business to change its processes, services and products to be competitive in the market. This change in business affects IT and requires new systems that could fulfill the new business requirements. Most of the organizations do not like to acquire IT so quickly due to budget constraints and therefore, applications are built using old technology or required functionality is added into the existing system which contributes problems in the systems.

Co-evolution needs to take place in business at all levels from macro level between organization and its environment (including businesses, customers, competitors and suppliers) to micro levels within the organizations. Any change at macro level affects various inter-related micro levels within the organization such as IT systems. This disparity between business and IT needs to be aligned properly so that the gap between both entities is reduced.

2.6 Business Processes Co-Evolution and NK Model

To describing business processes co-evolution, the NK model [64] is viewed a best approach where N can be considered as number of processes where each process is connected to K other business processes. Figure 2.12 shows an organization has 5 business processes (i.e. N = 5) without any internal connection (i.e. K=0). Each process is independent of other processes and can be adjusted for best behavior.

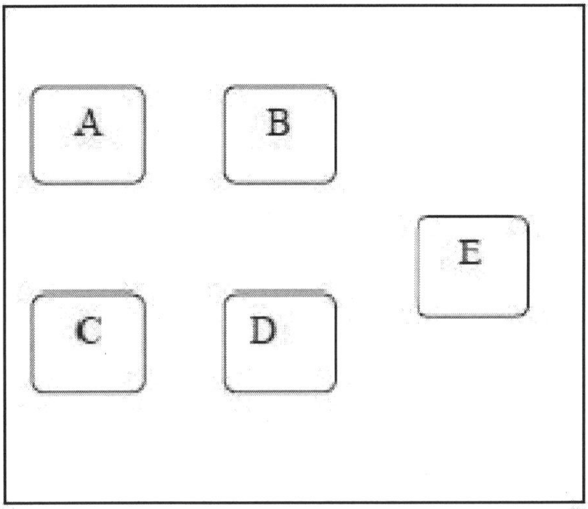

Figure 2.12 Processes are independent to each other [adapted from [28]]

When business processes are tightly coupled, a complex situation arises and in that case K = N-1. The figure 2.13 shows all the business processes are tightly coupled with each other and change in one business process will impact all other business processes within the organization. This shows co-evolution between business processes. For example, in figure 2.14 if process A does change all the processes B,C,D and E will also be affected since all are interconnected and transitive dependent.

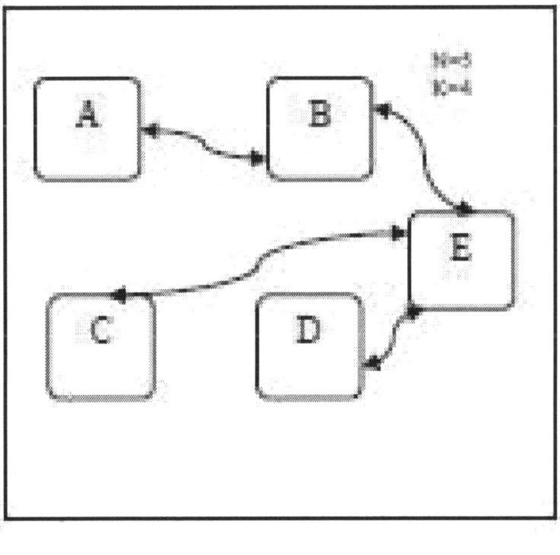

Figure 2.13 Processes are interconnected with each other

2.7 Related Work

Many researchers and practitioners have developed various approaches and frameworks to reducing the business-IT gap and increasing an alignment between the two entities.

A strategic alignment model presented by Henderson *et. al.,* [26] is a multidimensional model. This model has various dimensions that include strategic alignment, strategic and functional dimensions, internal and external dimensions. In this model 4 different alignment perceptions have been described. There are two perspectives 'strategy execution' and 'technology transformation', that are considered to be the drivers of the business strategy while the other two perspectives 'competitive potential', and 'service level', are thought to be the facilitator for IT strategy.

To address business and IT alignment a process-driven architectural framework [27] introduces and employs four-layer model for reducing the gap between business and IT. It is considered that there is a gap between the management of IT perception and practice. Therefore, this model assumes filling up the gap by:

- focusing on the business requirements and
- considering the information management carefully rather information systems or information technology.

Aversano [28] presented a coarse grained approach that is to be applied during evolution for misalignment identification between business processes and information technology. The misalignment occurs when any required changes are implemented. With this approach any additional change for any object is identified in order to restore the alignment.

This approach describes a technique for detecting misalignment by assessing a set of parameters between business processes and supporting technology. The requirements that need to be changed should be recognized carefully in order to keep the alignment attribute for aligned tasks and restoration of misaligned activities.

A Goal-Driven Development framework was developed by [29] for UML and MDA. The model helps organizations in aligning their business processes with IT. The business changes that are necessary for the business environment are identified in the business layer of the model and the goal structures. When changes in business occur their impacts have to be transferred throughout the business layer for organizational structures and later the impacts propagate to the application layer in order to synchronize with the IT structures. The goals are important to deliver observable specifications within business and application layers so that the impacts can be propagated between the layers.

Sabherwal [30] proposed a punctuated equilibrium model in which IT alignment goes through quick revolutionary changes. He suggests that alignment changes are small and evolutionary prevent any calamity by controlling misalignment.

Organizations consider the gap between business strategy and IT strategy a critical issue as it directly impacts on the business. Therefore, it is important to know the reasons for the gap between the two entities and a case study methodology [31] has been used to study the reasons. The study concluded that there was a gap between business and IT strategies in some targeted organizations. The research findings however cannot be generalized for other organizations.

Zedan [32] developed a framework 'K-Mediator' (Knowledge Mediator) that acts as a mediator between business requirements and underpinning technologies. The framework is knowledgeable of business needs and available IT assets within the organization. Basically the K-mediator role is to provide the means for business and IT evolution and managing their impacts.

The alignment between business and IT seems quite slow and rather static in the rapidly changing world. The business processes and IT functions can co- evolve with the passage of time. Now the companies who have invested a huge amount of money in information technology provide accessibility of their databases to their customers in order to customize their orders and keep track of the orders from manufacturing to the delivery. Companies are using IT to providing personalized services to their customers and to develop better customer relationship management. Therefore, business and IT are not only in alignment relationship and model, but they are in co-evolution relationship where business develops as the IT capabilities enhanced. [33].

Mitleton-Kelly [34] presented a hypothesis that problems with legacy systems could be reduced in result of co-evolution between business and IT. The base of the hypothesis is the assumption that the rate of co-evolution between two domains is affected by the degree and intensity of interaction of business and IT. This research found that a legacy system is not a function of age. A new system that does not fulfill user requirements and business evolution may quickly become a legacy system. This is due to the lack of communication and understanding between the two domains that leads both the domains to be evolved in different directions to create a business-IT gap. In this situation co- evolution rate between business and IT becomes low.

Benbya [35] viewed a business-IT alignment as a co-evolutionary process and presented a model based on co-evolution theory. The model proposes three levels of analysis (i.e. individual, operational and strategic). The framework that has multi-level aspects shows that IT is used in two ways in business. At one hand, IT has to fulfill the user's requirements and align with their needs i.e. IT is aligned with individual. IT also involves in the business processes i.e. IT has to be aligned at operational level. IT also plays a role in the strategies between business and IT strategies i.e. IT is aligned with strategic level. On the other hand, IT has to be aligned to the external environment. Co-evolution appears when a change in the external environment occurs requiring changes in both IT and organizational components.

Strnadl [27] has introduced a process-driven architecture (PDA) that is based on four layers (process, information, services and technology integration) and each layer attempts to bridge the gap between business processes and IT by using a nomenclature understandable to both business people and IT people.

Tivnan [36] supported co-evolutionary dynamics and agent-based models in organizational science in his study. Co-evolutionary dynamics occur at multiple levels of analysis within an organization (i.e. micro co-evolution) and between organizations and their respective environments (i.e. macro co- evolution). An organization's ability to macro co-evolve with its competitors depends on micro co-evolutionary processes [37].

McKelvey [38], in a research study, has described the management of co-evolution in detail and emphasized controlling the rate of co-evolution. The study elaborates damping mechanisms as methods of controlling the rate of co- evolution or shutting it down altogether. Given a co-evolutionary progression at some rate, there are two problems with the damping process: it occurs too quickly or too slowly. Most managers in organizations are unaware that positive co-evolution dynamics is suppressed by damping too quickly and negative dynamics is not suppressed quickly enough. One would like to know how to weaken damping mechanisms when co-evolution is adaptive and how to strengthen them when nonlinear order-creations get out of hand.

Morrison *et. al.,*[39] adopted the co-evolution term to describe the evolution of business and software at different rates. Then co-evolution was extended to accommodate wide-informatics systems that are assembled from parts that co-evolve with each other and their environment. A system evolves in result of internal or external factors that may or may not be expected ones. Such system has a dynamic co-evolution and a long life. The framework describes system's specifications, the executing software and the reflective evolutionary mechanisms within a single computational domain in which all the topics evolve in tandem.

Current Approaches for business-IT Alignment

Recently, different approaches for business-IT alignment have been presented by researcher and practitioners.

An empirical study has been carried out by Marcus *et. al.,* [137] in order to determine the alignment between emergency organizations and IT. They concluded that small emergency organizations do not utilize IT or do not manage properly. Although medium and large organizations are knowledgeable in strategic principles but they are not able to apply it completely or develop their processes. The study suggested a modular approach to enable strategic alignment in uncertain environments that could be beneficial for fast changing business environment.

To achieve business-IT alignment Aier *et. al.,* [138] have proposed an architecture-centric approach that separates external view of architecture from its implementation. In this approach complexity has been reduced allowing to be an ample approach for managing alignment.

Jan *et. al.,* [139] have supported enterprise architecture for business-IT alignment. They have presented a situation-based solution as situation varies from organization to organization. The business-IT alignment can be achieved by considering concrete qualities for business, IT governance and systems. Enterprise architecture meta-models for a situation is created to support the alignment.

A conceptual model-driven approach [140] has been presented for business-IT alignment. The approach aims at restriction of freedom in process modeling. A meta-modeling method has been introduced to support such restrictions.

A process-oriented approach has been presented by Tallon [141] for the alignment of IT and business. The approach aims at IT and individual process rather than business and IT strategies as one could assume.

A qualitative research conducted by De Haes *et. al.*, [142] presented an approach based on the use of IT governance practices (processes, structures and relational mechanisms) in different organizations. It was observed that the highly aligned organizations had more mature IT governance practices that implies mature IT governance practices lead to a better business-IT alignment.

Useful frameworks for our co-evolutionary framework

We discussed different frameworks above, but there are some frameworks that are useful to develop our co-evolutionary frameworks such as a model presented by Aversano [28] that helps to determine co-evolution in organization by measuring different parameters between business and IT. A 'K-mediator' framework developed by Zedan *et. al.,* [32] that acts as a mediator between business requirements and underpinning technologies. This knowledge mediator plays a central role in our co-evolutionary framework. Another model presented by Benbya [35] that is based on co-evolution theory is useful that shows multilevel aspects and the use of IT in business. Similarly Tivnan [36] supported co-evolutionary dynamics in his model and analysed organization at micro level to macro level. Morrison *et. al.,*[39] presented a dynamic co-evolution framework that helps to understand wide-informatics systems that are assembled from parts that co-evolve with each other and their environment. The work presented by McKelvey [38] helps to understand the co-evolution dynamics and the damping mechanism in organization. Strnadl [27] described layers (process, information, services and technology integration) where each layer attempts to bridge the gap between business processes and IT.

2.8 SUMMARY

The main purpose of this chapter was to review literature on various models in order to develop understanding for our proposed co-evolutionary framework. We found that different computational models may help developing the co-evolutionary framework for example, distributed parallel computing model may help developing co-evolutionary system in distributed environment in order to save time as evolutionary algorithms are useful for that. Since in distributed environment each task is considered as a software component, therefore, distributed environment may be useful for our co-evolutionary framework. Similarly client-server and component-based models may be implemented in our proposed framework. A comprehensive literature has been reviewed of business evolution and co-evolution of business and IT that establishes the foundation of our framework. A NK model of business processes co-evolution, but this model and it complexity will be discussed in following chapter. The chapter presented various alignment models, but almost all of them are conceptual models. It is found some models are directly related to the researcher's proposed framework such as [35] provides a multilevel approach in organization and a layered model that helps to understand co-evolution in organizations. A mediator model [32] acts as a mediator and in the proposed co- evolutionary framework it will help as a mediator to co-evolve both business and IT. It is also found that co-evolutionary process occurs at multiple levels within organizations and there are various parameters to be determined [28] for co- evolution. The chapter has helped in finding out useful frameworks that may provide foundation to the proposed co-evolutionary framework and the knowledge gained will be applied in the next chapters .

3

Research Methodology

A research methodology provides guidelines in order to follow and complete research study. This chapter describes the research methodology and research philosophy. The logical reasoning and two extremes of research philosophy have been discussed and positivism philosophy has been selected for its nature of empiricism. Co-evolution methodology and case study approach have been selected for the study and the respective reasons have been explained.

3.1 Choice of Methodology

The aim of this book is to present and explain a co-evolutionary framework in order to reduce the gap between business and IT. Keeping in mind this aim, the focus throughout the book will remain on various factors that affect the alignment between the two entities (i.e. business and IT). Therefore, the logical choice was the co-evolutionary methodology. A multilevel (i.e. different levels in organization) perspective will help to study the co-evolution rate between the business processes and IT. The co-evolution study at different levels such as at strategic level - business and IT strategies, at operational level – business and IT functionalities and at individual level – IT infrastructure with end users will be carried out to find out co-evolution between the two entities. A case study methodology is also a part of the research methodology used in this book. The case study approach facilitates to evaluate co-evolutionary framework in a financial domain.

3.2 Research Philosophy

Research is considered abstract and complicated, but if different phases of research are clear and well structured then it may not be that complicated. A research process usually begins with a broad area of interest and then research has to narrow down the question that can be studied in reasonable time using hypotheses. The research structure can be thought of as hourglass and figure 3.1 shows it. At the narrowest point of the hourglass the question in research is sought and later an attempt is made to address the broad question of interest by generalizing from the results of the study.

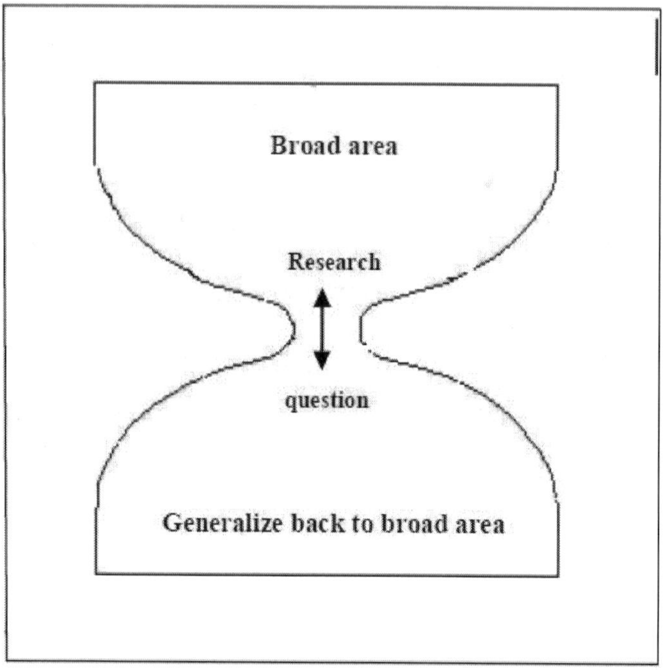

Figure: 3.1. An hourglass model

Philosophers used to call research 'logical reasoning 'and two major logical methods i.e. inductive and deductive methods are related to modern research [49].

3.2.1 Deductive Reasoning

This approach is used from a general to specific theory and is referred as 'top-down' approach. A theory is discussed in general that gradually narrowed down to specific hypothesis [49]. Figure 3.2 depicts hypotheses observations are collected that lead to test the hypothesis with data as confirmation of the theory.

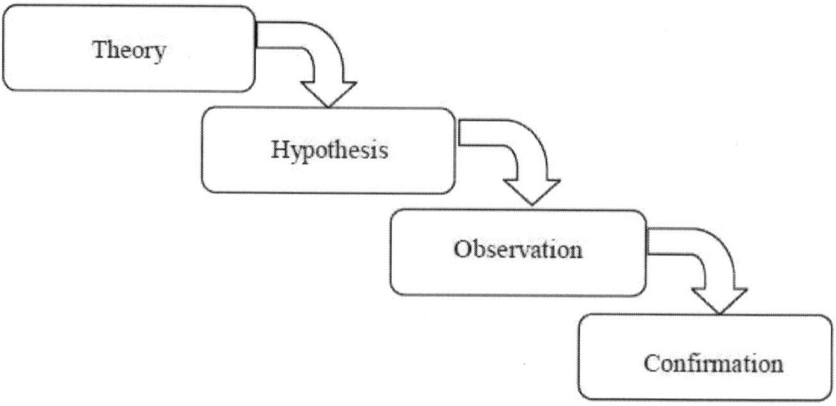

Figure 3.2. A deductive reasoning model

Deductive reasoning is narrow in nature and concerned with the confirmation of the hypothesis.

3.2.2 Inductive Reasoning

Inductive reasoning moves from specific to general theory and referred as 'bottom-up' approach. Specific observations are collected and then patterns are detected [49]. Some ad-hoc hypotheses are formulated that lead to general theory. Figure 3.3 explains this model

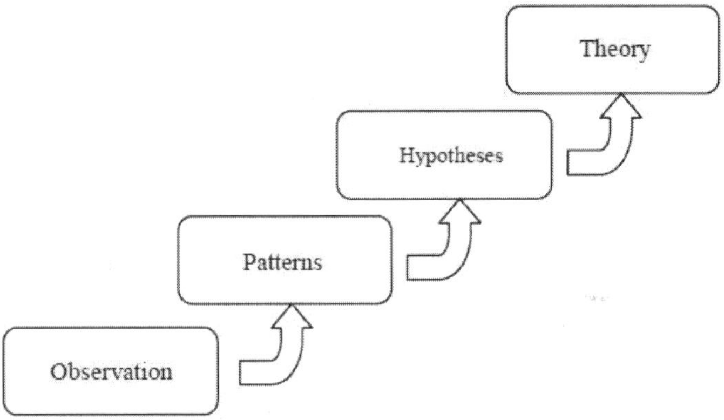

Figure 3.3. Inductive reasoning model

Inductive reasoning is exploratory and open-ended in nature.

Clarke [47] described research methods at different levels and considered the philosophical level as the basic research method. The general features of the world such as reality, reason, matter and proofs for knowledge provide the basis for postulates that relate to philosophical level of research method [48]. Proctor [49] indicates that it is important to understand the two extremes of research philosophy i.e. positivism and post-positivism before a decision of research method is made.

3.2.3 Positivism

Positivism states that the goal of knowledge is to describe the phenomena that one may experience and that knowledge beyond the phenomena is impossible. The basic reasoning of positivism presumes that the existence of objective reality is independent of human behavior.

A criticism on using the positivist approach is that in-depth human behaviours cannot be examined by any means. Parahoo [50] states:

> *"In physics, it is possible...to formulate laws relating to... the expansion of metal when heated. From such laws, the amount of expansion that will occur in particular circumstances can be predicted. However, when a man loses his job and becomes depressed, it does not mean that he will be depressed each time he loses his job, nor can we say that everyone who loses his job becomes depressed"* [50]

Humans are not 'objects' and subject to controls on actions, thoughts, insights and attitudes that positivism rejects considering irrelevant and belonging to mataphysics. Positivism is based on empiricism i.e. observation and measurement are the core of the scientific attempt.

This is useful for co-evolution study since this study will be carried out in financial institution, this philosophy provides opportunity to observe the insights of the organization and measure the parameters required to determine the co-evolution.

3.2.4 Post-positivism

Since the middle of the 20th century views in science have changed and especially a shift has been from positivism to post-positivism. Post-positivism supports the argument that scientists and common people think alike and therefore scientific reasoning and common sense are same process. Post- positivism rejects the basic principles of positivism. Now for post-positivism reality is creation of people involved in research and it does not exist in a vacuum. Proctor [49] indicates many factors that influence the reality such as culture, beliefs and gender.

A common form of post-positivism is critical realism which states reality is independent of thinking. In post-positivism critical realism all observation is imperfect and all theory is revisable. Therefore, it can be stated that post- positivism critical realism is critical to the ability to know reality with certainty.

The Post-positivist approach assumes reality is multiple, subjective and constructed by individuals. Multiple methods are used to study small sample in depth to establishing deserved claims as opposed to absolute truth.

3.3 Co-evolution Approach

The term co-evolution has been introduced by Ehlrich *et. al.,* [40] and in research context it is taken to mean that the evolution of one entity partially depends on the evolution of another entity [40][41][42][43][44][45]. In other words one entity changes in the context of another. Co-evolution takes place in an ecosystem and in biology an ecosystem means each type of organism has other organisms of the same type and of other types as parts of its environment [41]. In our research study an ecosystem consists of all related businesses within same and other types of industries that have impact upon and influenced by the organization under study. In a co-evolving system components of the system do replicate (contrary to evolution in biology where they do not replicate in terms of behaviour) that shows ‚a selection may act on the level of the parts of the system as well as on the system as a whole` [41]. Co-evolution affects both individuals and systems. When co-evolution applies to individuals and groups in an organization, it is considered as endogenous co-evolution and when an organization interacts with broader ecosystem, it is called exogenous co- evolution.

The co-evolutionary approach has been used in many areas from biology to economics and business to information technology [35]. Researchers and practitioners have been interested in co-evolutionary dynamics in order to improve the effectiveness on co-evolution process between the concerned entities. It has been believed for a long time that business strategies are analyzed and designed in such a way that IT applications and planning are aligned with the organization's objectives. But alignment between business and IT is not a state but a situation that unfolds in unforeseen manner, and therefore, any sudden changes or human errors cannot be included in any best planning. In any formal planning, at the strategic level, a flexible and creative strategy is significant and a detailed strategic plan to integrate business and IT strategy is important in order to reduce the gap to an extent. Business and IT strategy should co-evolve mutually to respond to changes in the business environment.

A multilevel perspective will help to study the co-evolution between the business processes and IT. The co-evolution study at different levels such as at strategic level - business and IT strategies, at operational level – business and IT functionalities and at individual level – IT infrastructure with end users will be carried out to finding out the co-evolution between the entities. In an organization's strategy evolution requires a continuous alignment with IT so that strategy is effective. It is important to study the relationship between entities at both macro and micro levels of interaction. Management of co-evolution rate has been described by McKelvey [37][38] in detail and used damping mechanisms methods to control the rate of co-evolution or shutting it down altogether.

Organizations need to adapt changes quickly for running business effectively or they may lose business. Co-evolution produces non-linear events [37][38] that at one hand they are good for the business but on the other hand they may be disruptive for the business. If little medicine is effective does not mean more is better. As long as co-evolution produces innovation and uniqueness in businesses it is good and this depends on the management to determine the efficacy of co-evolution. The co-evolution approach will help the researcher to determine the co-evolution at different levels in financial institution.

3.4 Case Study Approach

Yin [46] suggests a case is an empirical inquiry that investigates a contemporary phenomenon within its real life context using multiple sources of evidence. The philosophy of the case study approach is to obtain a complete picture of interaction of variables or events by looking a practical and real life situation. Some people argue that individual case cannot be generalized, but it depends on the type of case and the base how it is selected. A case study provides in-depth details, richness, and completeness [134]. A case study also helps to understand what causes phenomena and how and why the phenomena in the organization. The case study approach describes a complete situation as a combination of different factors. By using this method a number of properties and qualities can be established in a particular instance and may assist in determining the gap between business and IT.

Using the case study approach three different types of studies can be conducted. Firstly, an intrinsic case study that is undertaken for a better understanding on a particular case. This type of case study is useful when one needs to understand specific phenomena in an environment such as in our study we study co-evolution in a financial domain. Second type of case study is an instrumental case study that is carried out for refining a theory or examining a particular instance in more general manner. Third type of case study is a collective case study that is used to study different case studies in order to investigate a phenomena or condition [51].

For our research study we have selected the first two types of case study. As we are interested to study co-evolution in a financial sector that how it occurs at different levels and then we examine it in more general way. The reason for selecting case study approach is it helps the researcher to get close to the organization, gaining insights within the organization. As case study approach has extensive scope, the researcher may study co-evolution at individual and group level within organization. This approach also helps to understand the naturally occurring phenomena within organization such as the organizational environment, workflows and employees communication. For collecting data we will use multiple research methods approach [112]. This approach is useful for collecting data from different resources such as interviews, surveys and observations. Interviews provide opportunity to collect data directly from the concerned persons and any ambiguity can be clarified upfront. Survey instrument also a good tool for gathering required information and it is used when the respondents are dispersed or busy at work and unavailable for interviews. Observations provide opportunity to observe the working environment and the workflows of an organization. Sometimes survey instruments or interviews do not give the picture what observations can provide.

Therefore, to get comprehensive information for our study of co-evolution we have selected case study approach so that the co-evolution methodology can be applied and studied for developing our co-evolution framework.

3.5 SUMMARY

This chapter described the philosophy of research methodology and discussed different logical methods. It was found the deductive reasoning is suitable method to begin with our research because it provides a top-down approach. It helps to begin with a general theory and gradually brings down to the specific subject of knowledge. The chapter provided two extremes of research philosophy i.e. positivism and post-positivism. It was also found that positivism research philosophy is directly linked with the proposed study as the researcher intends to study co-evolution in real world i.e. empirically (empiricism or observation and measurements are the core of positivism). The chapter has presented a co-evolutionary methodology that is the base of the study. The co-evolutionary methodology helps to determine the co-evolution at different levels in organization. It is found the theory would help to study co-evolution in both the domains i.e. business and IT and it will help to develop co-evolutionary framework in an integrated fashion. The chapter discussed case study approach that is used to get close to the environment in order to get insights in organization. A multiple research methods approach for collection of data has been discussed and it will help to collect data in financial organization. Now these approaches will be used in the study and discussed in the next chapters.

Co-Evolution Model of Business Processes and IT

4

This chapter describes the co-evolution of business processes and IT. It also describes NK model of co-evolution of business and IT and its complexity. As the number of processes increase the complexity increases. The chapter explains how the complexity can be reduced. In this chapter requirements for co- evolution of business processes and IT have been explained in detail.

4.1 Co-Evolution of Business Processes and IT

Businesses have become more responsive to their customer requirements and needs. Enterprises worldwide are exploring new business opportunities by using advances in IT and increasingly reliant on its services. Initially the rudimentary role of IT was to improve the efficiency of business processes by automating manual processes. To support new business processes and to address challenges such as cost and complexity, firms are implementing strategies to manage IT services.

Now business processes are connected with the IT services, therefore, each business process is connected with two IT services (mentioned as dotted lines). There may be other IT services available to business process, but for describing the co-evolution process two different IT services have been considered. When a process is improved it may affect to IT services infrastructure which may, in turn, deform the process architecture. Hence in this sense evolution is a co-evolution.

If we consider the NK model again as stated in the literature reviewed earlier in figure 2.13, where business processes co-evolve now we add an IT infrastructure with N number of services and K connections between the services to support the business processes. The figure 4.1 shows the co-evolution between business and IT where 5 business processes transitively connected by 4 connections are supported by 2 IT services.

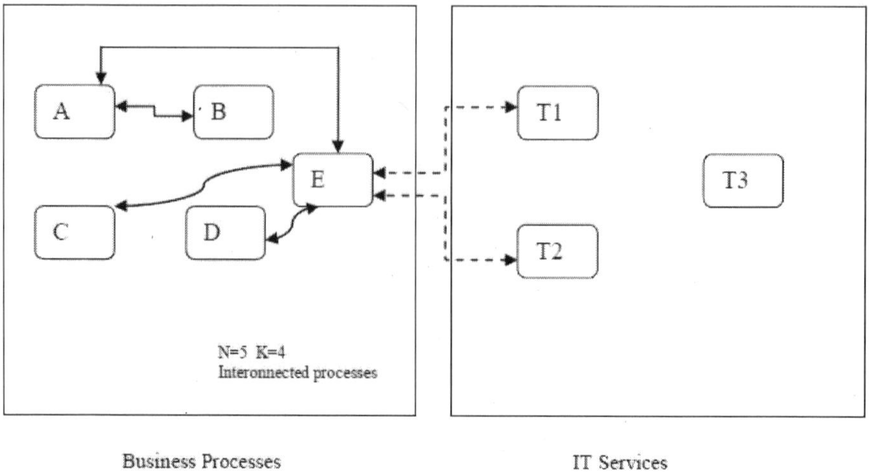

Figure 4.1 Co-evolution of business processes and IT

Co-evolutionary effects take place at multiple levels in organizations; therefore, it is necessary to understand the dependence relations among business processes and IT services.

4.1.1 Complexity

Organizations are focusing on aligning IT services with business objectives and attempt to optimize the performance of entire business organization. But as the number of processes N and interconnected links K increase the complexity of system increases. Complexity is a result of interaction and interconnectivity among different elements of a system [143]. In organizations any change or activity may have impacts on related components and the system. Connectivity applies to interrelatedness of individual elements within the system and relatedness between the systems. In figure 4.1 business processes (A to E) are interrelated with each other and related with the IT services.

Connectivity and interdependence among elements increase complexity, therefore, increasing business processes and interconnectivity in organizations create disturbance as a change in one process affects all the interrelated processes. If each process is given autonomy then the situation will be disruptive as processes would not know the each other.

Homann *et. al.,* [144] proposed a modular design to overcome such complexity by designing modular architecture in which components can be removed, configured and replaced in a dynamic fashion.

In viewing the co-evolution between business and IT, the modular design consists of business and IT subsystems that co-evolve in the environment. In a modular design both business and IT managers co-evolve the subsystems that may be due to user requirements.

4.2 REQUIREMENTS FOR CO-EVOLUTION OF BUSINESS PROCESSES AND IT

Information technology and business processes have been co-evolving for a long time. With the increasing development in the technologies the IT industry has become an essential part of businesses.

The business processes are supported by the underlying technologies and the technologies have increased the business growth and productivity. IT has increased the business efficiency by automating the business processes and caused for developing new business models. Businesses find new opportunities and requirements in response to the innovation in IT and similarly advancements in businesses require new technologies to emerge. Technologies have been innovating from the decades and businesses have benefited from the technologies in order to be competitive in the marketplace. Simply we can say that in today's world businesses are unable to expand and grow without using a complex technology and similarly, a multifarious technology is unable to innovate without modern businesses. Therefore, both business and IT co-evolve depending on each other.

Co-evolution of business processes and IT will help to accommodate changes in business process level and IT services level or vice versa [4]. In co-evolution IT should support the emerging business requirements on-the-fly but, it is not possible to gather all requirements and, therefore, IT should be adaptable for reconfiguration and at run time. To achieve such a dynamic configuration between business and IT, it is necessary to determine the requirements for business process modeling and dynamic business processes.

There are various requirements for business process modeling stated below:

a. A business process model should be user friendly in order to understand and automate processes without difficulty [65].

b. Since a business process is a variable process due to interaction by customers, vendors and other external entities, it is possible to experience uncertainties and therefore, business process model should be able to handle such uncertainties [65].

c. All business process models should be generic in order to accommodate changes in business and data flows [66].

d. Formal engineering principles need to be embraced by stakeholders so that a common understanding can be reached on business processes [65] [66]

e. All business process models need to be documented in order to have an accessibility to all stakeholders [66]

Business organizations always strive to provide best and efficient services to their customers, and IT is the tool that supports execution of the business processes [67]. The requirements for dynamic business processes are different than the requirements in traditional business processes due to the dynamic business environment.

Following are the requirements for dynamic business processes:

a. Dynamic business processes evolve in order to adapt new rules, policies or changes from customers. As a result of such changes new models evolve that help in co-evolution between the entities [126].

b. Since dynamic business processes constantly evolve for accommodating changes, the supporting IT services should be flexible enough to integrate new technologies or systems [126].

c. In a dynamic business environment, IT should be able to handle and control anomalous behavior and events where business processes are executed in a distributed environment [126].

d. In the event of new business collaboration, dynamic business processes should be able to make changes dynamically according to the new partnership [68].

e. In dynamic processes the working of a process is required to be protected from other processes and therefore it is necessary to introduce well defined interfaces [126].

f. Processes should have a loose coupling in order to minimize the propagation of any changes in one process to other processes [126].

In Figure 4.11 it is depicted that requirements are determined by business process models for organizations to design and deploy information systems.

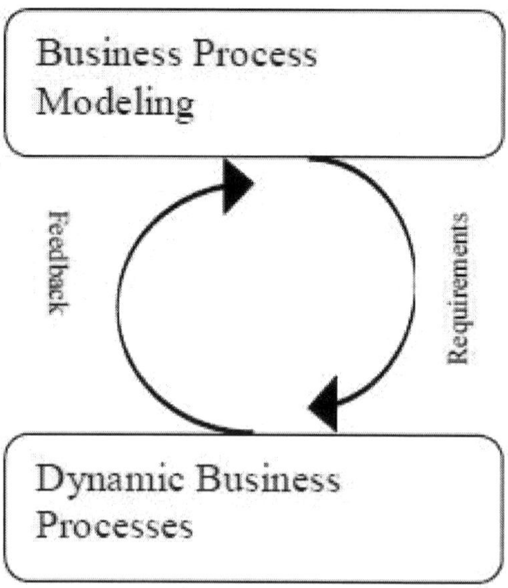

Figure 4.2 Co-evolution of business process requirements

As an example for the figure 4.2, consider a company has implemented a business process model based on the predefined strategies, policies and rules agreed by the stakeholders. If any of the stakeholders changes a given order or a policy or a new collaboration occurs then in this new requirement the dynamic business processes should handle this change and provide feedback to the business process model in order to update the model. This will co-evolve the business process requirements.

Changes in business processes, products and services always have an impact on IT infrastructure. In an intensifying competition organizations need to develop new products to respond market force. When new products and services are introduced existing system need to be updated in order to develop new functionality or new hardware. Therefore, evolution in IT requires business processes to be evolved and when both evolve at the same time then co- evolution occurs.

Co-Evolution Requirements

Following are the co-evolution requirements [38] between entities and if anyone of them is missing the co-evolution would not take place:

1. Agents (i.e. organizations, processes, entities) must be heterogeneous
2. All agents must be able to adapt any change to occur
3. They should be able to interact and influence each other
4. A higher-level constraint must be adapted in order to motivate co-evolution process
5. There needs to be an initiating event

4.3 Formalizing and Integration - Business Processes and Requirements for Co-evolution with IT

Alignment between business processes and IT should be considered during the evolution activities. When an object is modified a misalignment occurs that must be checked and appropriate actions must be taken. The change in the object may have impacts on other objects that can also be detected and based on their relationships suitable changes should be implemented. For example, to prevent a misalignment, a change in a business process may require changes in the software application that supports it. At the same time changes in application may require analysis and some changes in the business processes that are supported by the application. Identification of misalignment and measuring its level due to some changes in either business or IT domain is a major problem in keeping the alignment between business processes and IT. When changes are implemented in business processes a misalignment occurs between the business and supporting technology and a coarse grained strategy was described by Aversano *et. al.*,[28] in order to detect the misalignment. The strategy also identifies the object that need to be changed further in order to restore the alignment.

As stated earlier business managers and IT personnel need to have a continuous and coordinated communication in order to keep an alignment between business processes and IT services. Sometimes the inability of effective communication between business people and technical people causes a gap between the two entities. Sometime the technology works but the business processes are not aligned with the changes. Likewise, when business processes are ready to provide required services, the supporting technology is unavailable or does not comply as promised. When both business processes and supporting technologies are ready to deliver, unexpectedly either the business requirements are changed or external factors altered.

In an evolving system consistency is to be handled and when business processes and IT co-evolve, there is a need to understand the consistency relationship between both the entities. The business and IT entities are linked with a co-evolution relationship provided they interact with each other. The link established between the business and IT depicts the state of the alignment that may be current one or following the co-evolution process.

4.4 SUMMARY

The purpose of this chapter was to present co-evolution of business processes and co-evolution model and to discuss the requirements for co- evolution. The NK model of co-evolution has been elaborated and it was found that the complexity increases with the increasing number of processes and interconnected links among them. Any change in any component of business or IT affects other processes due to interconnectivity and therefore, this creates complexity in a system. The complexity of NK model can be reduced by using modular design architecture in which components can be added, changed or removed dynamically without affecting other components.

The chapter described the co-evolution requirements for business processes and IT. Requirements for business processes co-evolution expounded and it was shown that business process modeling requirements are changed with the dynamic business requirements. Therefore, it is important both business model and dynamic business processes requirements co-evolve in order to align with the supporting IT services. Finally the chapter described the integration of both business and IT and underscored the need of evolution in both the entities at the same time in order to keep alignment. A continually communication between the executives of both domains may keep the alignment. This alignment need will lead to construct our co-evolutionary framework that is discussed in the next chapter.

5

Architecture for Co-Evolution

This chapter begins with a review of related architecture such as business and IT architecture and discusses some alignment frameworks such as [77] that provides insights of alignment in terms of organizational patterns. These frameworks help to understand different layers in organizations. The chapter describes the proposed co-evolutionary framework in an integrated fashion where three levels of business and IT have been explained in section 5.5.

5.1 Review of Related Architecture

Recently business architecture has received much attention and emerged as a methodology and integral part of enterprise architecture [69]. Consequently, the concept of business architecture is vague and ambiguous and little research is found on the subject. Business models are considered as the foundation blocks for business architecture [69]. A business sooner or later will have a competition with the competitors; therefore they need to be dealt with appropriate strategies. Based on this fact some people consider that business model and strategy are interchangeable [70]. In support of this interchangeable notion people argue that Dell Computer introduced a new business model for selling computers directly to end users while other vendors sold by their resellers. This Dell's model not only saved the cost of value chain but also provided opportunity to knowing direct customers requirements and inventory management that other vendors were not able to do that due to their existing distribution channels. This business model worked like a strategy and benefited Dell for decade. However, in business architecture both business models and strategies are necessary.

We consider business architecture as a part of enterprise architecture that facilitates various business activities such as marketing, production, distribution, transportation, wholesale etc. We can say business architecture is composed of coherent functions of business, business objects or concepts and high level processes that depict working of business functions and objects in order to achieve the goals of organization. No business can be a successful without coherence among all the business functions. The business functions for examples,

Supply Chain Management (SCM), Customer Relationship Management (CRM), Marketing, Sales, Financial Management, Product Management etc. may work within organization, but as coherent functions they are linked and tied together to form a unit for achieving a common goal. For instance an effective marketing function brings a positive impact on sales. The Object Management Group (OMG) describes business architecture as a blueprint of an enterprise that provides a common understanding of organization and helps to align strategic objectives and tactical demands. In other words, business architecture lucid the structure of organization like capabilities of enterprise, strategies, business processes, structure of governance and information. Organizations implement strategies within available capabilities to execute business processes and ensure that information from all stakeholders (such as customers and suppliers) is properly managed.

Figure 5.1 shows a generic business architecture that is based on business strategy and all business functions such as sales and marketing, business objects that is intelligible entities such as customer and supplier and the business processes. Business capabilities (i.e. what organization can do or does) are executed by business processes that consider the flow of information by all business objects (i.e. external actors) and the supply chain.

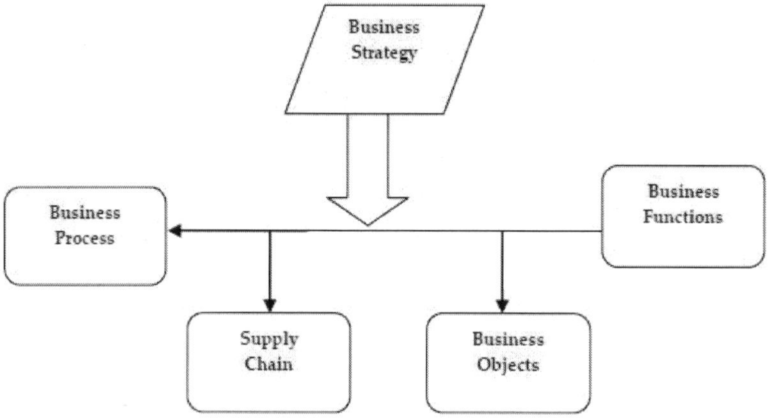

Figure 5.1 Business Architecture

The significance of the figure 5.1 is that it provides a layered view that helps to understand the layered approach. In our framework this will help to study the first level i.e. strategic level where business strategies are formulated to execute business processes.

5.1.1 Business Strategy

A business strategy defines future direction and scope of an organization to achieve benefit by configuring resources in changing environment in order to meet the needs of market and stakeholders' expectations [70]. Business strategy is the basis of a business architecture that consists of elements like organization aims and objectives that state the future goals of the company and measureable targets to be achieved by employees. Another element of business strategy is business case that provides reasoning for a project initiation; for example, an organization may upgrade its running software for performance improvement, but as a business case this improvement may develop employees' performance to satisfy customers' needs.

Strategy is formulated based on the strategy statement that describes aims, objectives, mission (i.e. statement of the role the company has) and vision (i.e. statement of future where the company will be). The strategy statements are arranged at different levels in terms of their significance. For example, statements that describe the scope of company and its business, vision, mission and marketplace are at the top level while statements that are limited in scope and specific based on higher level are placed at lower level. Individual statements are related with each other and the outcome of individual statement provides insight to company. Consequently, business architecture gets more details, introduces new levels and new domains (i.e. cluster of business functions and objects). At this point strategy becomes clearer and better understanding of the strategy is evolved.

When business architecture is created all the decisions are directly related to the elements of the strategy that helps understanding the significance of maintaining domains. Business architecture aids in organizational structuring in which business domains and their responsibilities are assigned. The assigning of domains to individuals such as top managers causes development of other architectures since the owners of the domains are directly involved and responsible for their respective domains.

5.2 TECHNOLOGY ARCHITECTURE

Organizations are increasingly dependent on technology as it has become a driving force. As the new businesses requirements arise or new technologies emerge organizations experience pressures and they need to respond to these external pressures. Organizations and their business processes are implemented and supported by an infrastructure of software and hardware that is said to be technology architecture. Technology architecture describes the structure and relationships of the technologies that support the business operations within organization. Technology architecture describes a systems design of software applications and sub-systems that are interlinked with each other [71]. The architecture is considered as a blueprint that guides and explains how technology and information work together and efficiently achieve the goals of an organization.

Technology architecture supports security and reliability to applications, but if the applications are not designed to avail benefit of technology architecture then applications perform poorly. Likewise, a well designed application that has been implemented by reusable components may not perform properly if the technology is improperly configured. This shows a relationship between technology architecture and application architecture. Figure 5.2 (adapted from [72]) illustrates the relationship between the technology and application architecture. The figure shows the functional requirements are input to application architecture and at this stage technology architecture is also built. Application development defines the deployment rules and policies and at this stage operation of data center is begins that are integrated through network devices.

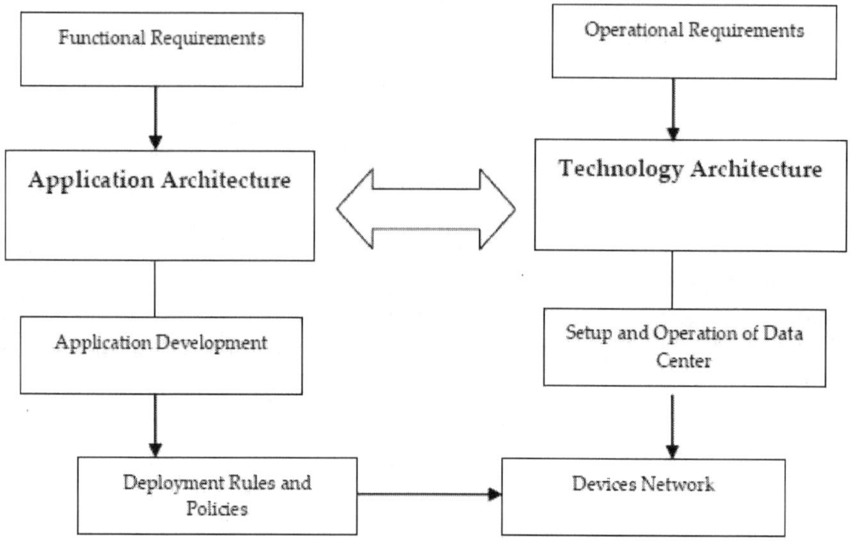

Figure 5.2 Technology-Application Architecture

5.2.1 Application Architecture

Application architecture describes the design of an organization that includes software application, sub-components and external applications. Software applications fulfill the business requirements and rely on underlying operating systems and databases. We consider application architecture as a blueprint that ensures the underlying modules of an application will support expansion in future. The expansion can be in terms of resources or requirements.

Examples: The 'distance' between business architecture and application architecture

Organizations experience a 'distance' between business architecture and application architecture that affects on the business. For example, a growing manufacturing company decided to begin with e-documentation in order to facilitate stakeholders for convenience, speed and easy location of the documentation. The company started searching the tools for developing the required web based system, but the unavailability of the required resources forced the company to select the web based solution from outside. The solution, however, could not fulfill the requirements completely as it was expected. The solution was unable to control the workflows and monitor and audit them. Since the decision of the solution was IT based, business requirements could not be gathered properly due to miscommunication or misunderstanding. From a business perspective, the solution turned out to be less effective in the business processes and inflexible for to be tailored to meet the business requirements. The company needs to reengineer the existing system and acquire the tools for in- house development. A delay in implementing new business process is better than acquiring a solution that does not fulfill the business requirements.

A tour company is using a booking system developed in-house in a mainframe environment. The system was developed in obsolete technologies and in terms of application architecture it is very difficult to maintain such a system due to paucity of skilled professionals in those technologies. As the business grew the company needed to buy new software in order to move everything from the old to the new system. From the business view point the company has a flexible and scalable system that could meet business requirements and they can introduce new products in the market immediately (like discounted holiday package). The company could get advantage over its competitors provided the competitors are not using the same package. The right solution for the company is to reengineer the existing system for implementing the required functionality. It has proved easier to delay without doing anything rather than adopting another system.

5.2.2 Architecture Views

The architecture has multiple views that usually referred as conceptual view, logical view, physical view and implementation view. These views are determined by the requirements. Figure 5.3 (adapted from [72]) shows architectural views.

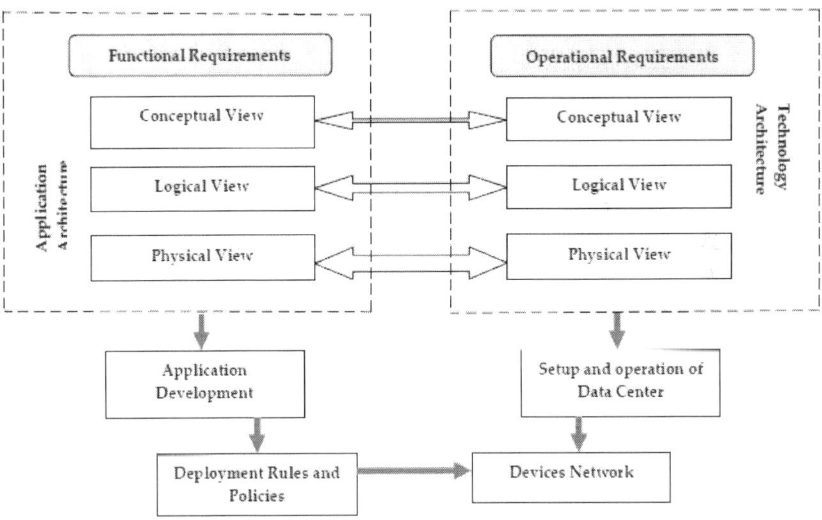

Figure 5.3 Architecture Views

Conceptual View

In technology architecture all technology areas are described and defined in order to develop an understanding of the required technology among stakeholders. This ensures that required technology areas are fully understood for implementing the functional and non-functional requirements and available within the organization.

In application architecture business models are built based on the business requirements and description of key business processes is developed.

Logical View

The technology architecture describes the main functional elements and their relationships that are needed for the operational requirements in organization. In application architecture application models are designed in which data management and processes are mapped and interaction among different parts of the models is depicted.

Physical View

The physical view of technology architecture shows mapping of elements to the real technologies in terms of both software and hardware. In this view complete technology architecture with required technology such as operating systems, databases, servers, network devices etc. are implemented. In application architecture the physical view realizes the application model into implementation model. In this view coding is done but major infrastructure of distributed applications and data is controlled by frameworks.

5.3 ENTERPRISE ARCHITECTURE

Enterprise architecture describes the enterprise business objects and their relationships with external environment, organizational goals, business processes, principles governing its design and evolution. It also states the organizational structures, software applications and computer systems. Enterprise architecture has four different layers that are commonly accepted in overall enterprise architecture [73]. Figure 5.4 shows the four layers (architectures) of enterprise architecture.

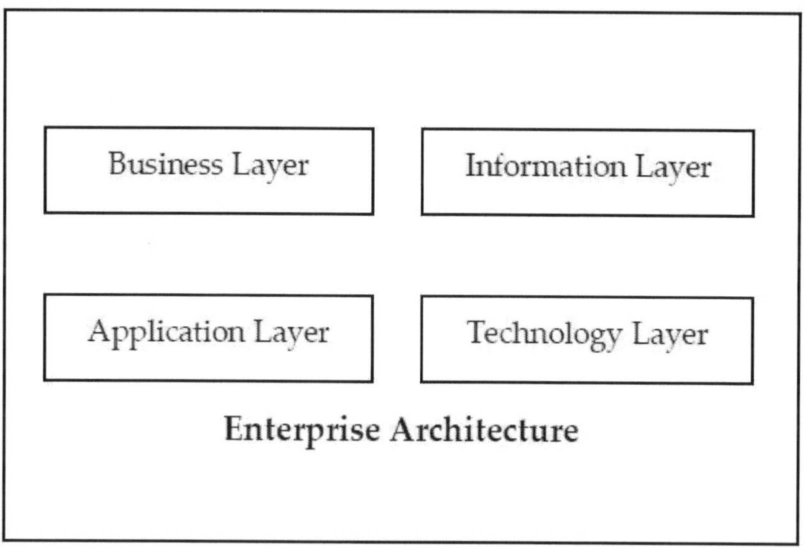

Figure 5.4 Enterprise Architecture Layers

- The business layer represents the organization of company in viewing the business strategy. This also defines key processes such as customer-supplier relationship processes, organizational goals, offered products and services, and targeted market [70][74].
- The application layer presents the blueprint of application systems and their relationships. It also shows the interaction with the key business processes of the organization [75].
- Information layer represents the structure of logical and physical data management resources of the organization. It also shows how information are organized and secured.
- In technology layer software, hardware, operating systems, database management systems, telecommunication and network devices are organized that are essential in deployment of applications.

Enterprise architecture has been successful in supporting decision making for changing in business. Since enterprise architecture is composed of business models and technical models, the impact of any change within organization or/ and in business process can be noticed on supporting systems.

This has been noticed in recent years organizations are taking much interest in enterprise architecture rather traditional architectures such as technology and application architectures. The reason is continuously changing market worldwide that coerces organizations to bring structural and strategic changes. Enterprises and researchers are focusing their attention towards enterprise architecture and discuss its strategic impacts [73]. Enterprise architecture framework is a management tool that facilitates organizations to obtain the maximum benefits from both business processes and supporting IT by bringing them into an alignment. It is a comprehensive framework that helps for aligning enterprise's processes, people and IT resources. We can say enterprise architecture describes the supporting role of information and technology in business processes to acquire business benefits.

Traditionally IT has been playing a back office role, but now IT is evolving its role to formulate new business strategies for enterprises. Organizations are trying to find out the reasons for not achieving the anticipated return on investment in IT; and they are always in search of alignment theories and methodologies in order to attain the alignment between business and IT. There are various architecture frameworks have been developed in order to align business processes and IT; first we would discuss few architecture frameworks that aim at aligning business and IT and later we will develop our co- evolutionary framework for reduce the gap between business and IT.

5.4 Architecture Frameworks for Aligning Business and IT

A changing business environment causes a business to change its processes, services and products to be competitive in marketplace. This change in business affects IT and requires new system that could fulfill the new business requirements. Since financial constraints do not allow technology to be replaced or updated, applications are built on old technology or required functionality is added into the existing system which contributes problems in the systems. The widening gap between business processes and supporting IT systems is attributed to the misalignment between business processes and IT. The misalignment is caused due to separate design of both business processes and IT systems [76].

5.4.1 Strategic Alignment Framework

Henderson and Venkatraman [77] presented a framework for aligning business and IT in which they proposed IT alignment in terms of organizational patterns and scope that are dependent on IT. The strategic alignment framework recognizes the potential of IT in shaping business policy. When we look the model carefully we see the business and IT areas divided in four different components. Figure 5.5 shows the framework.

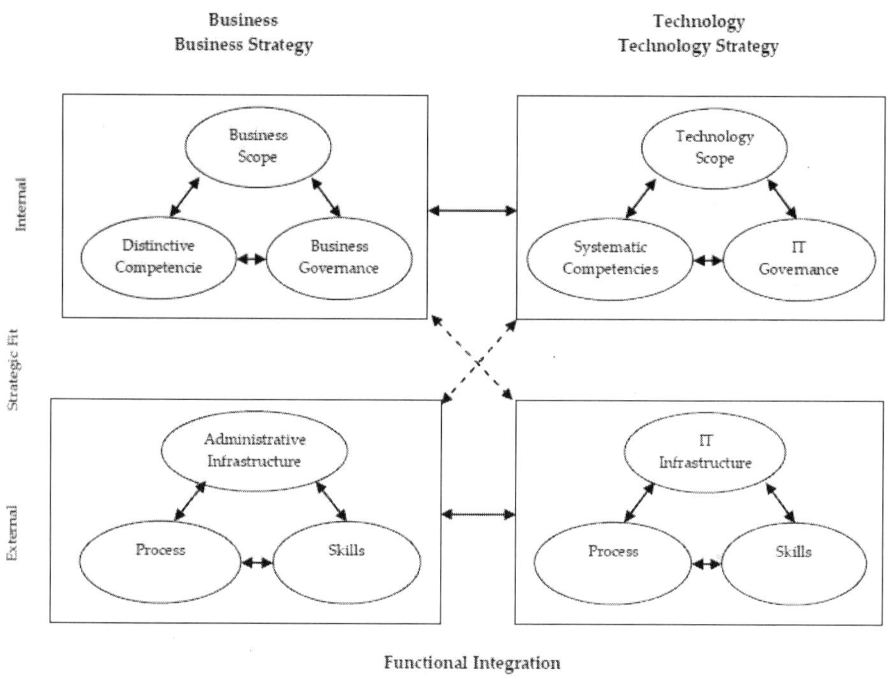

Figure 5.5 The Strategic Alignment Framework [77]

The above model demonstrates the alignment between business and IT in two aspects; i.e. the first aspect is strategic fit (i.e. alignment) between external and internal domains and second aspect is functional integration between business and IT domains. The model emphasizes the role of IT and its strategic significance in formulating business strategy.

The above framework mainly concerned with technological and organizational infrastructure and processes where the horizontal dimension shows direct cooperative influence of business and IT. It shows that the strategic level is prevalent and main director in the relationship of business and IT. But there are other factors that contribute in the business-IT relationship such as finance, culture and politics. Therefore, organizations should be information prone in order to share and use it internally and externally [78].

5.4.2 Integrated Architecture and Unified Framework

The framework presented by Henderson and Venkatraman has been adapted by Maes [78] that is shown in figure 5.6.

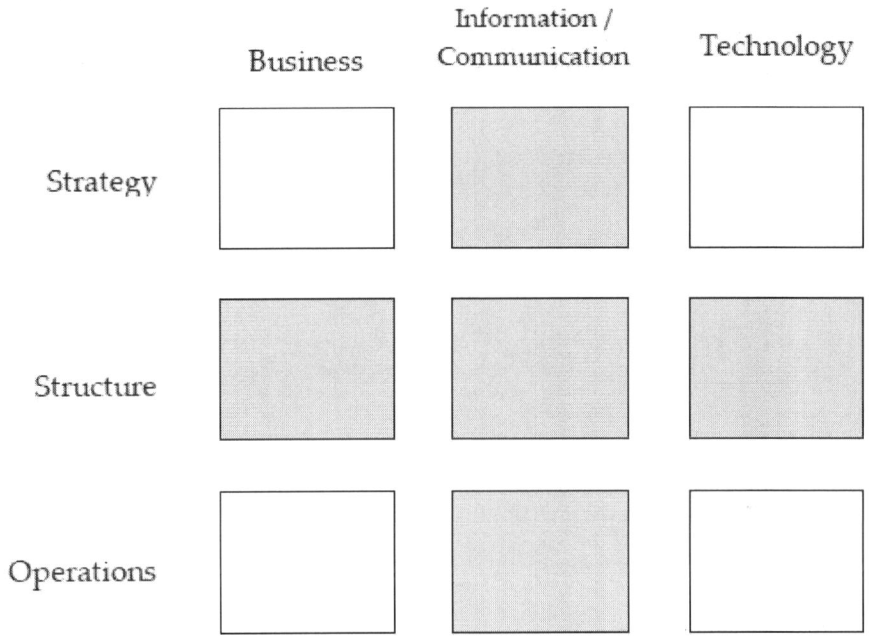

Figure 5.6 Framework showing business-IT relationships [78]

In figure 5.6, the framework shows business-IT relationship where row 'structure' and column 'information/communication' are the variables that can lead to an alignment of business and IT. Maes *et. al.,* [79] introduced the Integrated Architecture Framework (IAF) that supports integrated architectural design of business and IT which is an input for business and IT alignment. The alignment of business and IT does not only automate the business processes but enables enterprises to introduce new products, new services, building customer relationships and creating new channels. The IAF comprised of architecture areas, design phases and specific architecture viewpoints. Figure 5.7 [adapted from 79] depicts these dimensions.

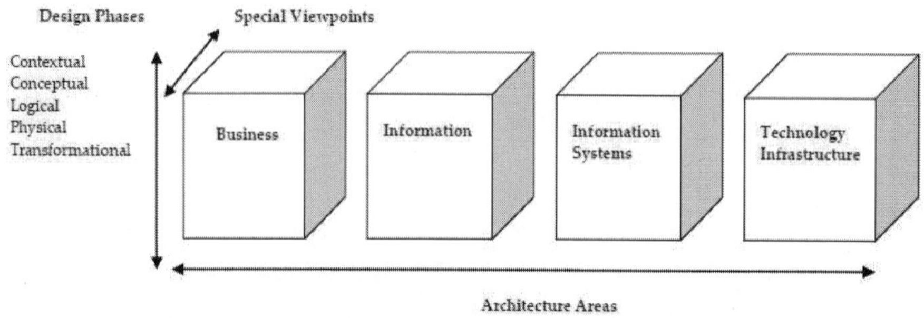

Figure 5.7 Integrated Architecture Framework (IAF) [78]

When we compare both the frameworks shown in figure 5.5 and figure 5.6, it is apparent that the technology column in figure 5.5 is divided into two columns in figure 5.6 i.e. information systems and technology infrastructure. The information systems column represents the software component while the technology infrastructure represents hardware system. Similarly, when we see the rows in figure 5.6 and figure 5.7 it is obvious that in figure 5.6 rows represent the levels of management while the rows in figure 5.7 show different phases of design process. The Strategy level (row) in figure 5.6 corresponds to the Contextual design phase in figure 5.7. The next three phases in figure 5.7 are the elaboration of Structure level in the framework in figure 5.6 while the last phase i.e. Transformational in figure 5.7 describes the operations and implementations of information system corresponding to the Operations level in the figure 5.6.

In result of the amalgamation of both the above frameworks, a new unified framework [79] emerges that consists of management and design components shown in figure 5.8.

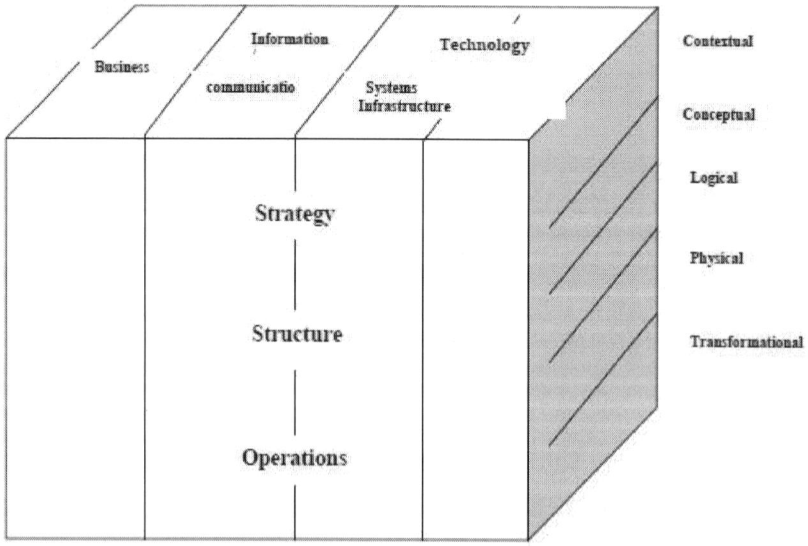

Figure 5.8 Outline for a Unified Framework for Alignment of Business and IT [79]

The framework outline in figure 5.8 shows that the alignment is a combination of management and design concerns. This unified framework deals with the issues concerning architectural and information sharing. The alignment is considered at individual level and its concerned variables. The 'strategic' alignment at strategy level depends on the concerned variables such as governance, scope and mission. Similarly, the 'structural' alignment depends on its variables such as capabilities and architectures. The 'operational' alignment at operational level depends on processes and skills. All these variables need to be aligned both horizontally and vertically.

5.4.3 Mechanism between Business and IT

Organizations improve their decision making and agility by integrating business and IT. We have already discussed that business architecture focuses on strategy and the relevant processes. The application architecture facilitates services that are defined as applications and implement the defined business process and model. This application architecture defines the user interaction with the application such as internet, mobile device or portals. Then technical architecture or technical infrastructure implements the application architecture which shows the mapping of processes on software and hardware. Figure 5.9 shows the mechanism between business and IT

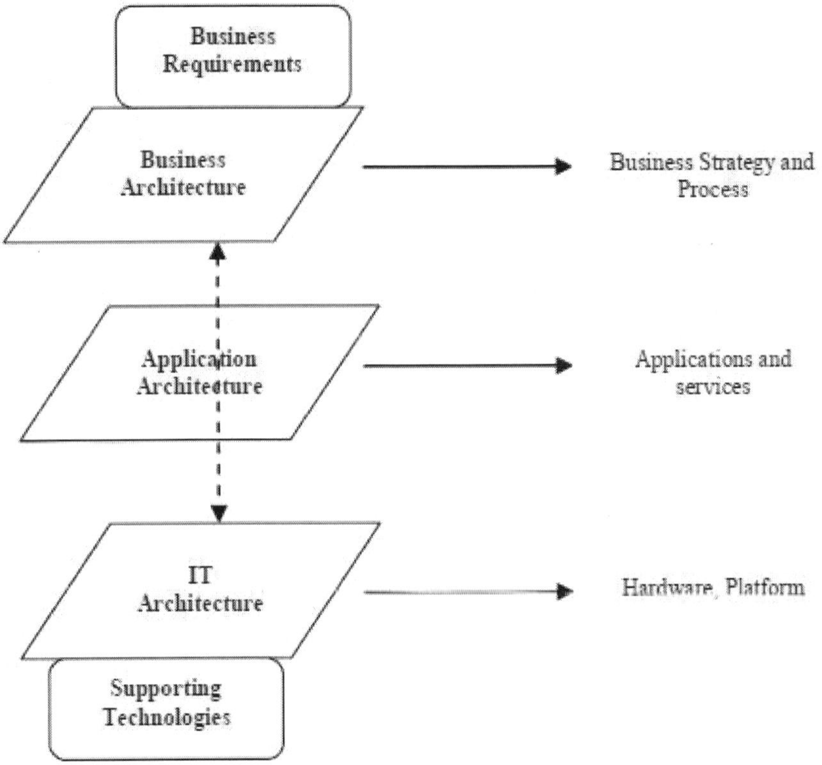

Figure 5.9 Business - IT mechanism

Figure 5.9 shows that business processes and strategy are used to distribute the services to customers and become essential parts of applications. IT assets are examined in order to implement the functionality required by the application layer. To work the mechanism properly and to have an alignment between business and IT, it is important to ensure that the IT architecture implements the business processes properly. Business processes lead the development of IT solution and consequently alignment can be achieved.

5.4.4 Role of Strategies in Alignment of Business and IT

In today's world businesses are investing in IT but without focusing on its strategic use. Since IT has a potential to change enterprises, it is important that IT is used in effective manner in order to align the IT strategies with business strategies. The success of every business depends on the alignment of business and IT strategies. Strategies implemented in one organization may be adopted or imitated by other organizations and, therefore, strategies need to be adapted in order to keep alignment within organization. Organizations strive to develop business processes in order to achieve competitive advantages. Companies always evaluate their strengths and weaknesses in order to determine position and strategy to be adopted in the marketplace. It is also significant to organizations that the supporting IT resources are properly managed and organized in order to support any changes planned for future. The IT resources include software, hardware and human resource that ensure the future change is in-line with the corporate aims and objectives. To achieve alignment, it is necessary that IT is positioned strategically in the corporate structure. This ensures that business strategy has the latest supporting technologies and the required services. An appropriate strategic IT planning is useful in aligning with the business processes that help to find out new opportunities [80]. In order to align IT with business processes top, management of organizations need to understand the benefits of alignment. Business and IT executives should consider the importance of IT as an integral part of business and develop mutual understanding. Strategic alignment can be enhanced provided the business executives and IT executives are in communication and share the domain knowledge. Reich *et. al.,* [81] suggested that for strategic position of IT within organization requires professional from both domains (i.e. business and IT) should be knowledgeable in both domains. Business professionals must know the IT-related activities and managers should participate in technology-oriented events. Likewise, technology personnel should move to business units and attend business events in order to understand the business processes and their functions. In a competitive environment organizations strive to align both business strategies and IT strategies but to achieve alignment is difficult especially when the coupling is tight between the two entities. It is important that the business and IT strategies are aligned in order to reduce the widening gap between both entities. The reducing gap will improve the efficiency and develop relationships with customers and suppliers. The inverse of this will result in failure in investment, loss of business credibility and failure in recruiting and retaining skilled resource.

5.5 ARCHITECTURE FRAMEWORK FOR CO-EVOLUTION

The architectures frameworks discussed above aim at aligning business and IT, but none of them discussed the alignment in view of co-evolution as both business and IT evolve independently. We argue that when organizations change their business strategy in order to evolve their business processes, the supporting technologies are not evolved. Likewise, when IT infrastructure is evolved or new technologies are introduced in organizations, the business processes are not evolved, consequently, a gap is created between business and IT.

Co-Evolution: It is the term used to describe the relationship between business and IT that are changing dynamically. A business system becomes relatively unstable in result of change in business process requirements and in turn, the supporting IT services are affected. If the IT does not adapt to supporting the new business change, the business loses efficiency and effectiveness. Similarly, when the new technologies are introduced in organization but business does not alter accordingly then it loses its effectiveness and competitive position in the marketplace. Therefore, such mutual relationship between business and IT is known as co-evolution.

Static co-evolution: This process occurs when the system goes off-line in order to make required change in the source code, recompile and re-link with the data. This process may require long down-time of the system that organizations cannot afford as some important data encapsulated in components may not be available. Therefore, essentially a system should be up all time even during the evolution of the system.

Dynamic co-evolution: This process evolves a system as a part of its execution and therefore, does not require down-time. A dynamic co-evolution system is unstable as it evolves in response to any internal or external drives.

Our co-evolutionary framework is based on dynamic co-evolving system that is comprised of business and IT entities. In dynamic co-evolution it is important to ensure that in result of any change in business, the supporting IT also evolves. A process is adjusted by an open system in response to an environmental input [82]. The dynamic co-evolution needs to be open system in order to get influenced by unpredictable changes. In our proposed co- evolutionary framework we understand there should be monitoring mechanism that could check the requirement either for business or technology so that co- evolution process occurs. Zedan *et. al.*, [32] developed a framework 'K-Mediator' that plays a role of mediator between business and information technology.

K-Mediator

The K-Mediator is knowledgeable in both business needs and the supporting technology assets in organizations. It can have first-hand knowledge of business requirements that need an IT solution; this makes it more important than an architect, requirement engineer or domain engineer since these can make errors in expressing requirements. Figure 5.10 shows that in results of internal external environment and events such as politics, business tactics, finance and strategies the impact is analyzed as k-mediator is knowledgeable in both domains.

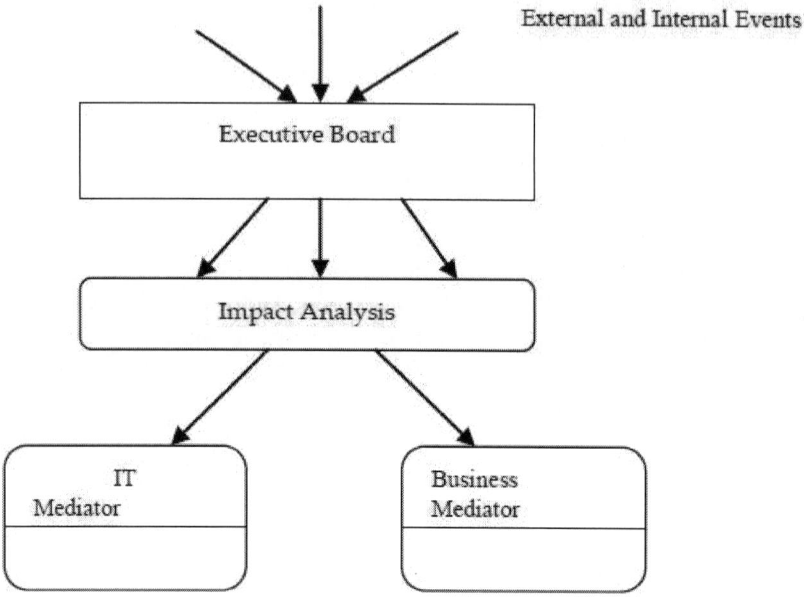

Figure 5.10 K-Mediator

The computation unit of K-Mediator is component that encapsulates services which are accessed by interfaces. A component contains two types of services i.e. 'provided services' and 'required services'. Provided services have set of features while required services contain components for performing services. A general form of a component defined in K-Mediator [83] as below:

COMPONENT CName

PROVIDEDSERVICES:

[pr1] A: (f11...,f1n; f21,...,f2n,...)

[pr2] B: (g11,...g1n; g21,...g2n,...)

REQUIREDSERVICES:

C: (h11,...,h1n; h21,...,h2n;...)

D: (i11,...i1n; i21,...,i2n;...)

END CName

The mediator is an important part of our co-evolutionary framework that is responsible to monitor the requirements and create or compose the required components. Figure 5.11 illustrates the co-evolutionary framework that shows three levels of business and IT and their components such as strategy, rules, policy, departments, software, hardware etc. All levels are integrated by K- mediator that facilitates co-evolution of business and IT.

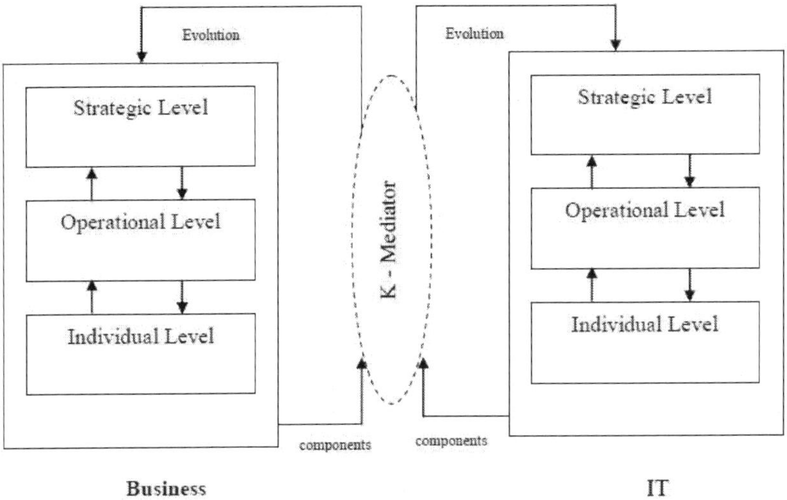

Figure 5.11 Co-Evolutionary Framework

Our three-level co-evolutionary framework consists of the following levels:

1. Strategic Level
2. Operational Level
3. Individual Level

Strategic Level

At the strategic level both business and IT strategies co-evolve. Companies manage their business processes and deliver products and services to their customers. At times companies need to adapt business strategies in order to be competitive and effective in the marketplace. As the business strategies are changed IT strategies must be changed in order to support business processes. This will be achieved by the knowledge mediator (k-mediator) who is knowledgeable in both the domains. It strategies are formulated based on the information that come from the business processes. IT strategic planning is based on the information and therefore, a thorough understanding of business strategy and company structure is significant.

Both business and IT strategies are linked and when both the strategies are matched organizations develop core competitiveness. It is necessary to understand the business strategy and the relationship with IT strategy. The IT strategic planning encompasses network architecture design, security architecture systems and load of equipments. It provides a secure and reliable IT strategy for the business development. Therefore, at the strategic level business and IT strategies are co-evolved as the k-mediator is always there in order to achieve co-evolution.

Operational Level

A tight coupling between business and IT requires a continuous coordination and communication between the two domains. Business executives and IT planners need to understand each other's requirements in order to build successful links between business objectives and the IT architecture. At this level software applications and related components fulfill the business requirements that rely on underlying operating systems and databases. People from both business and IT must discuss and develop an effective collaborative partnership at all levels. Business processes are functional and deliver the services and products to customers. The IT resources are used to support the business processes in order to meet organization's objectives and therefore, operational performance at all levels is important.

Individual Level

A system or IT architecture may not be effective unless if fulfils the user's requirements. The individual's requirements change drastically and therefore, it is necessary to involve users in the development process. As the users are comfortable using systems innovations and new ideas arise and that requires changes in the system. In result of new business process or new service or product a change is required in order to meet the user requirements. Co- evolution occurs at all levels to accommodate changes in the system.

In our framework the K-mediator plays a central role all levels that inputs requirements into an IT repository where a Knowledge Base supports the requirement as the concerned business. The mediator checks the IT asset in order to find available component(s) to support the requirements or create new ones (i.e. evolution in IT). If components are available then composition of the components fulfills the business requirement otherwise new components are to be developed and integrated. Hence, the system co-evolves with the change in business requirement and its IT solution.

In our dynamic co-evolutionary system it is necessary that the system partially halts during its execution in order to decompose its constituent parts and create either new components or evolve existing components to form a new system for execution.

5.5.1 Dynamic Co-Evolution Process

A co-evolving system always changes from one state to another as it evolves due to interaction with its environment. When a requirement (i.e. a change) is needed the system transforms from existing form to the new state. This change in behavior of the system depends on the behaviour of the participating elements/ variables of the entities.

In our architecture, the co-evolving application is constructed based on the following requirements:

1. An operator to halt the system execution (partially) in order to decompose its constituent parts
2. An operator to scan the system for providing representation (source code) of the evolving system
3. A method to convert the representation to a new representations
4. An operator to compile the representations and bind into running system

Now we explain below that how these requirements for co-evolution are satisfied.

5.5.1.1 Composition and Decomposition

We know application construction depends on the composition of different components for computation. For example a financial application may have components such as accounts receivable, budgets and analysis, cost accounting etc. As a result of composition they execute in parallel.

For a dynamic system evolution, it is essential to decompose a running system into its constituent parts and recompose following evolution of the components or creation of new components without changing state or data.

To describing this process, we consider a client-server system of three client components that are in communication with a server component. This is depicted in figure 5.12

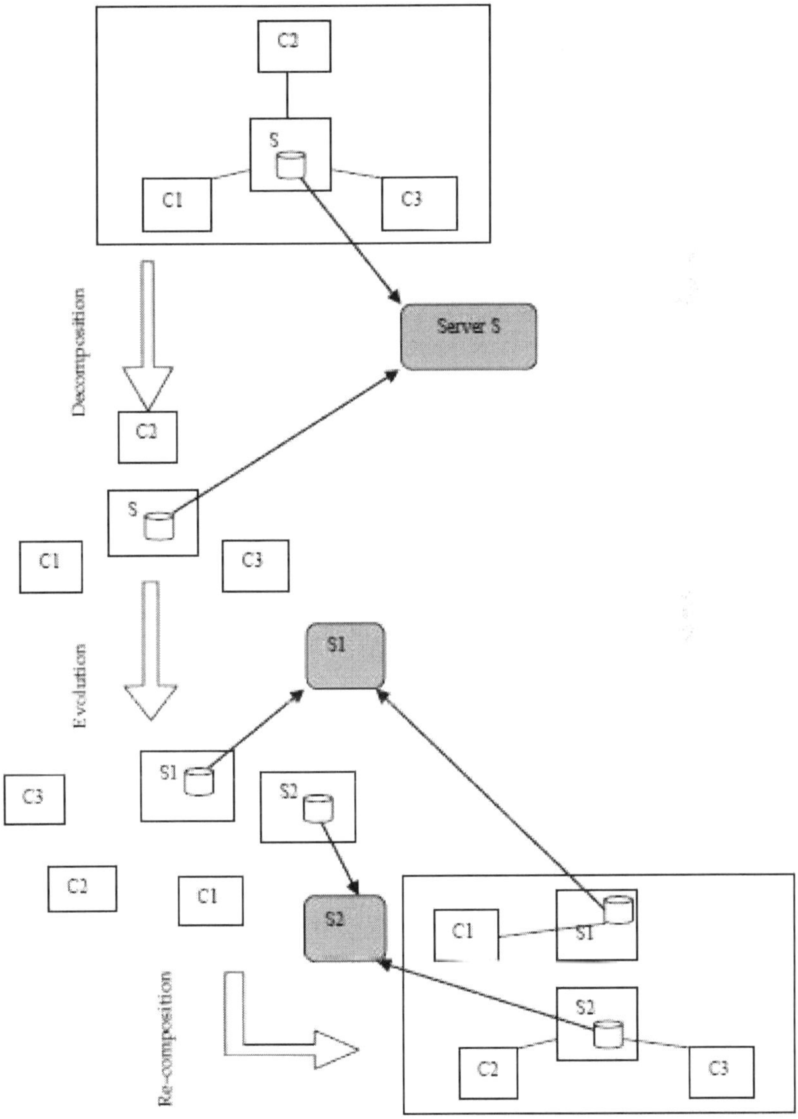

Figure 5.12 Composition decomposition process – System Evolution

Consider there are three client components c1,c2 and c3 and a server component s1 that provides data to the clients. We assume client c1 needs quick data service from the server component and this requirement arises into the system. The system will be checked to see if required component can provide that service or not. To evolve components first links are broken while the server component maintains the link with the data as depicted in the figure 5.12 (decomposition). The server component is divided into two components that still maintain the link with the original server as shown in the figure (evolution). In result of evolution in the server component all five components re-compose to form a new system as the figure 5.12 shows it (re-composition). Now the client c1 component has a link with one server component and two other client components have a link with another server.

5.6 Summary

The main purpose of this chapter was to present proposed co-evolutionary framework. The chapter reviewed related architecture and frameworks that present the layered structure. A business strategy is the core of business architecture and the chapter has presented business architecture and explained business strategy. The researcher has constructed a business-IT mechanism that show business processes and strategy are used to deliver services to customers and become the part of applications. In order to implement functionality IT assets are examined. This mechanism provides knowledge of different levels and helped to understand co-evolution at each level. In this chapter the researcher has proposed a co-evolutionary framework that consists of three levels in business and IT. Co-evolution occurs in all levels by means of k-mediator as it understands the requirements of both the domains. The chapter contributes to knowledge in a ways that the co-evolutionary framework using k-mediator has been presented in an integrated fashion where co-evolution can be studied in three levels i.e. strategic level, operational level and individual level. Each level has its own components and the co-evolution occurs within each level. The proposed framework is a unique in a sense that all three levels co-evolve with each other with the help of k-mediator. This co-evolutionary framework has a potential to enhance the performance of organization and is likely to generate more revenue as the co-evolution expedites the business processes. This framework is evaluated and validated in a financial institution and next chapter explains it.

6

Case Study and Evaluation

This chapter presents a case study of a financial institution in order to determine co-evolution within the organization. Since the case study is for financial organization therefore, description of some e-commerce models has been given that are usually used in financial institutions. To evaluate the proposed co-evolutionary framework data collection and analysis techniques and methods have been explained. The chapter describes how data of different items of business and IT in the organization validates the framework.

6.1 Financial Sector

The financial sector is the most complex among many business sectors that provides various products and services to customers, from small account holders to giant corporations. The financial sector has gained maximum benefits of the technologies and provided their services to customers. Now from retail banking to stock exchange all available on internet. Internet has become an essential channel for delivering financial services that transformed traditional approach of 'bricks and mortar' into a 'click and mortar' one [86].

6.1.1 E-commerce Models

Now financial services and products are delivered by e banking that are more convenient and faster for customers. Mobile banking is also becoming increasingly popular among customers and financial transactions are performed using mobile phones. The financial sector is facing challenges of e-commerce and some adjustments have been adopted according to the banking requirements [87] [88]. In e-commerce different models are used to offer e-commerce services to the customers [89].

6.1.1.1 Business to Consumer (B2C)

In this model consumers interact with the business organization to purchase products/services via an interface that consists of information technology such as software, network and telecommunication connection.

The figure 6.1 shows such a model

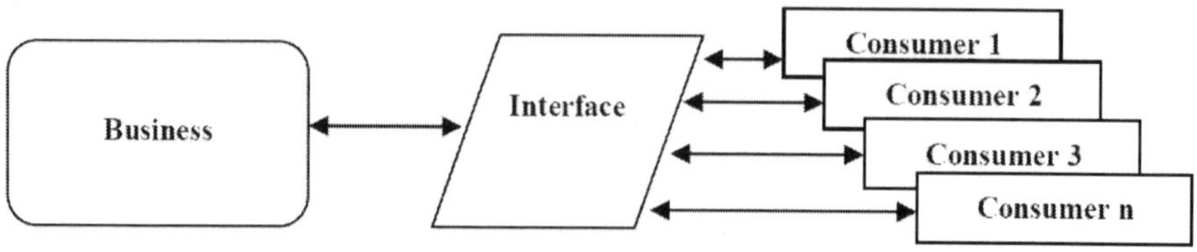

Figure 6.1 Business to consumer model

6.1.1.2 *Consumer to Business (C2B)*

In this model consumers strive to sell their services and products to business organizations and in search of businesses where services are required. Figure 6.2 shows this model.

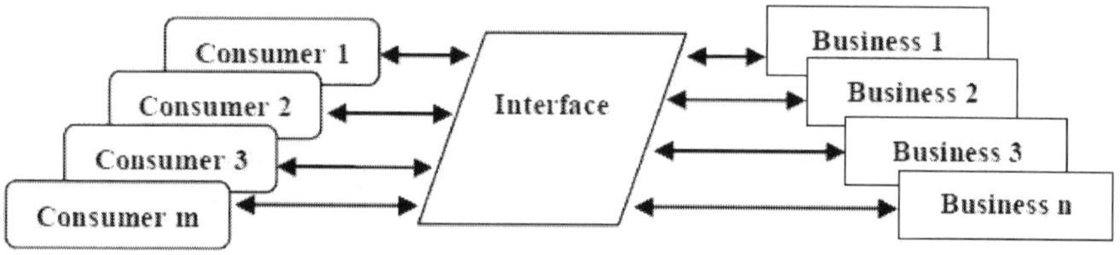

Figure 6.2 Consumer to business

6.1.1.3 *Business to Business (B2B)*

In this model business organizations exchange data electronically and banks make transactions online from each other. Since both buyers (business) and sellers (business) interact with each other, the relationship is business to business relationship that is represented in figure 6.3.

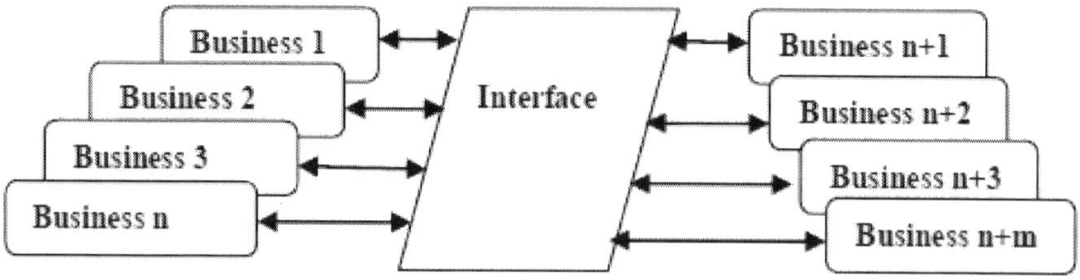

Figure 6.3 Business to business

Private sector had recognized the importance of this model in e-business and e- economy earlier [130].

6.1.1.4 *Consumer to Consumer (C2C)*

In this e-commerce model customers (consumers) sell and buy products or services to other customers online such as auction. This is represented in figure 6.4.

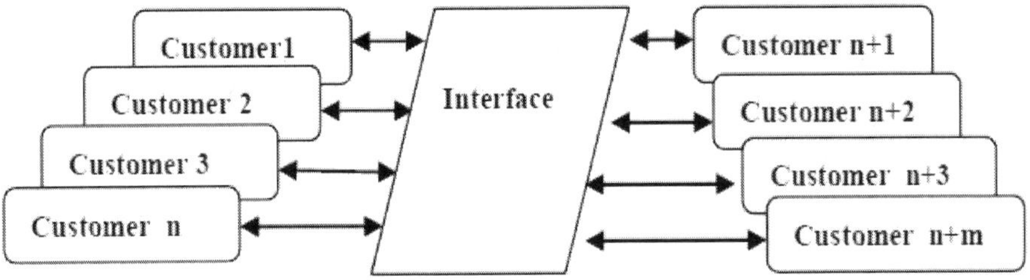

Figure 6.4 Consumer to Consumer

In financial institutions two models of e-commerce from the above (i.e. B2C and B2B) stated models affect the retail banking and investment banking. The major technology vendors such as Sun Microsystems, Microsoft, Oracle and IBM facilitate the implementation of e-commerce in banks [90].

6.1.1.5 *Business to Consumer Model*

In banks customers buy different banking products and services through the interface that consists of software, network and telecom connections. Consumers may purchase the services regardless their account within the same bank. The model is depicted in figure 6.5

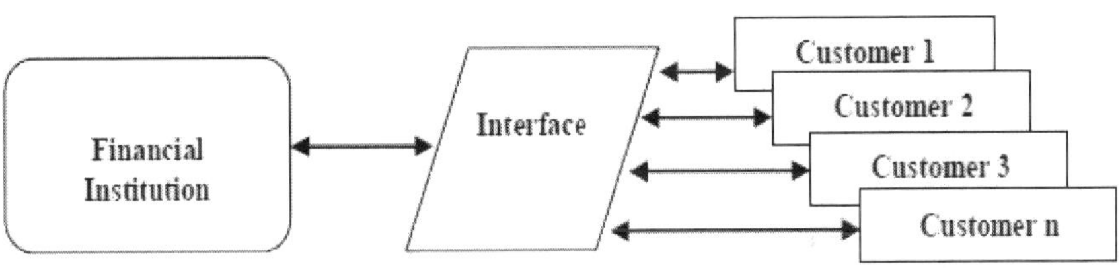

Figure 6.5 Business to Consumer model in bank

6.1.1.6 *Business to Business Model*

In banking systems this business to business relationship is used to exchange data and complete daily routine procedures among banks from one to another. This relationship expedites the process, saves cost and other resources. The figure 6.6 shows the model

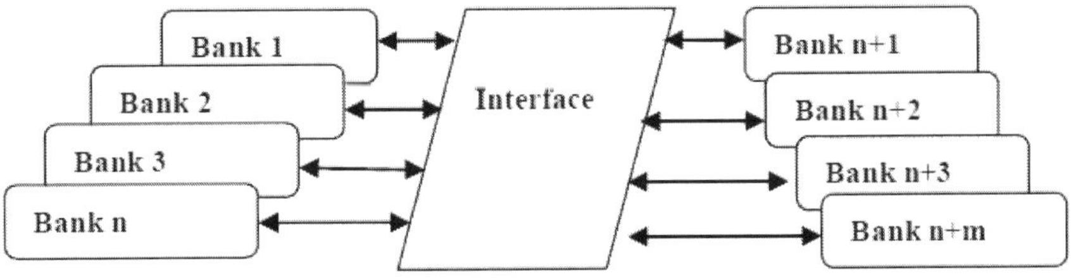

Figure 6.6 Business to Business model in banks

In banking business both the above relationships (i.e. B2C and B2B) are used to establish connection between customers and bank and banks to banks in order to make transactions and exchanging data. During the processing of business transaction data is settled according to the B2B relationship between the participating banks.

Financial sector is growing rapidly that is supported by the development of information technology. Besides internet banking (i.e. E-commerce) other services such as ATMs, telephone banking and mobile banking etc. are being offered by banks.

6.2 EVALUATION OF THE FRAMEWORK

We have selected the financial sector for two reasons. First, the financial industry is a dynamic one that always strives to meet the customers' demands that cause changes in business functions. Secondly, financial institutions are always keen to adopt technologies for providing efficient and effective services to the customers. We are interested in different measures and dimensions of a system in the financial domain in order to determine the co-evolution of business and information technology in the financial institutions. Financial institutions adopt technologies to expedite the business processes in order to improve the performance of organization. However, researchers realize that there is a complex relationship between IT and organizational performance [91]. When organizations announce investments in IT they receive a positive impact [92], but actual returns from IT investments are insufficient and experts suggest that there is a little evidence that IT investments have positive impact on measures of organizational performance [93]. We would evaluate organizational performance in order to determine whether IT has co-evolved the business processes and vice versa. We will use objective and subjective data for evaluating organizational performance. The objective data refers to the financial data such as return on investment (ROI), return on assets (ROA), internal rate of return (IRR), net present value (NPV), sales growth, revenue growth etc. whereas subjective data calls upon the perception of the respondents [94][3].

6.2.1 Data Collection and Preparation

There are four methodologies of empirical research in information systems areas namely case studies, laboratory studies, field studies and field tests [95]. We selected ABC Bank (due to privacy agreement we hide the identity), one of the largest financial institutions in Saudi Arabia that has expanded tremendously due to its innovative and effective services and products. The ABC has set an example for being a well aligned company that has started developing business applications, retains employees and provides excellent services to its customers. The ABC Bank has hundreds of branches and a range of products and services to offer to its customers. We contacted to the ABC head office and explained the reason for conducting the research study and requested them to identify the departments and the concerned decision makers who were knowledgeable in both business and information technology.

The ABC Bank provided us with documents in the areas of information systems, business plans, enterprise architecture and organizational performance etc. The ABC executives and managers provided us with the comments and views in various interviews and discussions of up to one and half hour duration each time. We prepared our questions for interviews, but occasionally the data was collected in form of questionnaire due to unavailability of the concerned people. The questionnaire approach is useful in obtaining quantitative scale and qualitative data [96]. The survey method is inexpensive, less time consuming and simple to collect data from dispersed audiences. The survey research is defined as a collection of information for scientific purpose from a sample of population using instruments [97]. In addition to interviews, a survey approach has been chosen in order to exploit the following advantages:

1. It is believed to be an economical method to examine a complex phenomena [98] .
2. Survey instruments document norm, identify extreme outcomes and describe associations between variables in a sample [99].
3. Survey instruments give good results of independent variables on dependent variables [98].
4. The research instruments provide more systematic data than case studies and facilitate generalization [100].

However, there are some problems with the survey research and they have been considered as below:

1. An excessively large survey instrument may create problems in administering and analyzing data. Surveys with 12 or less number of pages may expect a reasonable response rate [101].
2. Large sample sizes may give researcher a wrong perception in evaluating statistical significance. It is important that in a large sample smallest relationship may yield statistically significance differences at acceptable levels of reliability [102][103].

6.2.1.1 Ethical Considerations

In any empirical study ethical considerations are important and we also kept such considerations before the inception of the case study. The participation of people in the study was completely voluntary and participants were informed the objective of the study for higher learning. All participants were assured that information would not be made available to anyone who was not directly involved in the study and there anonymity would be preserved. To ensure that no verbal information was missed out, we audio taped the participants and before doing that we had asked the permission from the participants. The participants were allowed to edit their conversation on tape or even they could have withdrawn from audio taping during the interview process. In all cases the tapes were erased after the data had been transcribed.

6.2.1.2 Data Collection Method

There are different methods of information collection such as face-to-face, email, mail, telephone and web. Selection of methods depends on the financial resources and circumstances [104], we have used a mix of the methods i.e. face-to-face, email and mail. We used telephone to clarify any question and to following up the survey instrument. In this modern technology world we also mailed out the survey instruments in order to access otherwise inaccessible people and flexibility to reply to the questions we intended to ask during face-to- face meetings.

6.2.1.3 Response Rate

The quality of findings of a survey research gets affected by its response rate [105] as the low response rate may not be considered a reliable and generalized data [106]. Response rate can be increased by giving incentives to the respondents; for example, personalized cover letter, statement of confidentiality, a precisely written questionnaire, simple and clear instructions etc. [107].

We have interviewed executives and managers in business and IT departments and other employees face-to-face in order to collect information. At times we were not able to meet directly with the concerned persons and in that case we used our survey instrument to collect the information we intended to ask during the face-to-face meetings.

6.2.1.4 Survey Instrument Design

When a survey instrument is designed there are some factors that need to be considered carefully such as type of the questions, format, content and classification of the questions [108].

Types of questions are termed as open-ended and close-ended where open- ended questions provide respondents an opportunity to describe their views in narrative form. Although open-ended questions give free hand to respondents to reply in their own words, the drawback is difficulty in administering the questions and difficulty in data analysis. Usually respondents refrain replying such questions as they require significant amount of time. In viewing this we did try to keep such questions in a minimum number in our instrument. The close- ended questions, however, are easy to manage and for analysis. Respondents are given various options to select the best one according to respondent's opinion. Close-ended questions are like multiple choices, true/false, yes/no, ranking and rating scales type questions. Likert scales are used in the rating type of questions where respondents select the level of agreement in a specific statement. Likert scales are useful in empirical studies that are related to adoption of information technology [109]. We used a five-point scale in our survey instrument as it is adequate for subject-centered scales and used in research of adoption of information systems technology [110][111].

Content and Classification of the questions either in face-to-face meetings or in survey instrument has great impact and effectiveness. If the questions are designed and constructed in clumsy manner they may lose the real essence of the questions leading to unwanted results. When we constructed the questions we kept them brief and clear in order to be read and understood completely. We classified our questions in categories concisely and clearly for example, business strategy, technology strategy and overall organization performance. We did try to ask one question at a time in an item of interest; for example, if the respondents were asked whether the business strategy was 'effective and aligned' with technology in one question, we may not be able to get the right answer whether it is about effectiveness or alignment or both.

Considering the terminologies in both the domains i.e. business and IT, we avoided the jargon so that questions and their meanings are clearly understood by the respondents.

Non-response items may result in wrong and incomplete data that may adversely impact the reliability of the survey instrument. A respondent may opt not to response of any item for some reasons such as:

a) The questions may not be relevant to the respondent's field of interest or domain

b) Respondent does not understand the questions and consider them as vague

c) Respondent may not feel comfort in replying the questions.

d) Respondent does not find the required option from the given ones in order to reflect his true answer

In our questionnaire and face-to-face meetings we requested that the respondents to reply to all the questions without leaving anyone of them blank. In case of any ambiguity, misunderstanding or query in any question, the researcher made available himself for clarification and helped them by any means. Non-response questionnaires (i.e. any single question without answer) were eliminated from the study.

6.2.2 Survey Instrument

The survey instrument is based on the interviews questions. As we stated earlier that the instrument was designed to collect data from the executives and managers who were unable to meet in person for one reason or another. The questionnaire comprised of four sections.

The first section of the instrument aims at measuring the overall performance of the ABC and, therefore, required variables have been measured in this section such as annual budget, sales growth, operational cost, return on investment etc.

The second section of the instrument focuses on the measurement items for business and IT strategies. A large number of questions measure the IT role in business strategy, business growth, impact of business process reengineering, business competitiveness, audit of business architecture, innovation in IT, audit of alignment strategy, IT architecture, IT budget etc.

The third section consists of mix of open-ended and close-ended questions that are related to architecture in ABC. In this section we are interested that respondents explain the environment and discuss the architecture of the bank whether it has been reviewed and updated. This section also collects data about the technologies being used and their impacts on the business processes within the bank.

The fourth section of the instrument determines the background of the respondents i.e. gender, age, education, management position, experience, annual income etc.

6.2.2.1 Measurements of the Items

Our literature review helped to identify the definition of business and IT strategies and relevant variables including the organizational performance. We identified the items and concerned variables for our interviews and survey instrument. For the instrument we have used a five-points Likert's scale where the range of responses is from 'Strongly Disagree' to 'Strongly Agree' with a middle option as 'Neutral'. A respondent opted 'neutral' to indicate the middle response between either agree and disagree or neither agree or disagree.

Therefore we have used typical Likert's scale (with the numerical values) to represent our data i.e.

SA = Strongly Agree (5)

A = Agree (4)

N = Neutral (3)

DA = Disagree (2)

SDA = Strongly Disagree (1)

6.2.2.2 Measurements of Organizational Performance

We know that organizational performance depend on various factors within and outside of the organization. Many researchers have found that IT has great impacts on the performance of an organization [113][114][115][116]. To measure this dependent variable we used different items that are given in table 6.1

Table 6.1 Items to Measure Organizational Performance

Item	Expression
FPS	The organization has increased the number of financial products and services within last year
ASG	The annual sales growth position is remarkable as relative to the competitors
CS	The level of customer satisfaction has increased as compare to the previous years
OC	The operational cost within organization has decreased
MS	IT has facilitated our organization to gain market share as compare to competitors
RS	The organization always rewards to staff based on the business performance
OI	The image of the organization has improved
QPS	The quality of financial products and services has increased
ROI	The organization has excellent rate of return on investment
IRR	In our financial institution any new launch of product or service has a good internal rate of return

6.2.2.3 Measurements of Business and IT Strategies

In ABC the performance of the company is affected by various factors, but we are interested in the business strategies, IT strategies and the IT environment including the architecture that is being used in the company. Our measurement items for business and IT strategies are listed in tables 6.2 and 6.3 respectively.

Table 6.2 Items to Measure Business Strategies

Item	Expression
BSIT	In our organization IT has a significant involvement in shaping our business strategy
BSP	IT people should be engaged in shaping up the business strategy
BRIT	IT role in the organization is to support business processes
BOGT	The organization is growing due to implementation of technology
BMIT	The business managers should consult with the IT managers in preparing business strategy
BPRO	The business process reengineering should be a routine work within our organization
BPAS	The personnel of our organization is well aware of business and IT strategies
BART	The organization reviews and updates the business architecture in result of any IT innovation
BSPC	Our organization offers new services and products to be competitive in the industry
BOR	The organization is willing to take risks

Table 6.3 Items to Measure IT Strategies

Item	Expression
TICS	IT investment in the organization is linked with corporate strategy
TA	Our organization acquires state-of-the-art technology (i.e. software, hardware) as soon as the need arises
TBA	In the firm IT budget is restricted and considered as an expense rather an asset
TLB	IT people have difficulty in understanding business requirements due to the lack of business knowledge
TUR	The information systems are updated as soon as new business requirements are introduced

6.2.2.4 Data Coding

The data we collected from ABC through interviews and survey instruments from require meeting the analysis requirements i.e. entering data and coding in a proper format.

The responses we received either from the direct interviews or in survey instruments we re-coded for each question. We used the conventions stated in [107] that describe the coding process for assigning numerical value to every answer of each question in the study. For example, when we asked the question about respondent's gender we coded 1 for male and 0 for female. Likewise, we entered numerical values for all the answers we received against each question in the interviews and the survey instrument. The numerical values become the attributes for the variables.

6.2.2.5 Data Entry

There are different means of entering data into computers such as keyboard, scanner and bar codes. We used keyboard to enter data into Microsoft Excel and used some statistical tools and software such as SPSS. Before entering data into spreadsheet, we checked the data thoroughly as any mistake could lead to unwanted or incorrect results. We ensured that the data entered was verified in order to enter the quality data into the spreadsheet. We removed any errors in the data, for example, in the open ended questions we carefully recorded answers and extracted the real essence of the response. By real essence means the exact information relevant to the question avoiding unnecessary details. We also verified the codes entered are according the answers given by the respondents.

6.2.2.6 Test for Reliability

The reliability of a questionnaire is significant in extracting the results and, therefore, we wanted to ensure that each item in our survey instrument was reliable. An item is said to be reliable when it produces the same results from the same object [119]. Internal consistency is an important aspect of reliability that shows consistency in the measuring scale [120]. To assess the internal consistency of a measure the Cronbach's coefficient has been used and [121] suggested that set of items should have a coefficient alpha equals or greater to 0.70 to be considered internal consistent, however, alpha value greater than 0.60 also shows internal consistency [104][122].

In the survey instruments and interviews we found all the items with alpha coefficient values in the range of 0.67 to 0.72 that show reliability of the data.

6.2.3 Data Analysis and Results

During the interviews, observation of the documents provided by the banks and the data collected through survey instruments we found that the enterprise architecture of the bank is reviewed annually by the management and technical division of the bank. The aim of the architecture development was to maintain the consistent alignment between business processes and the supporting technologies.

The new products and services to meet the requirements of the customers exploit innovation in technology that causes a change in the architecture. We found the enterprise architecture of the ABC bank is composed of two main structures i.e. business and technology. Each structure consists of various components and the table 6.4 shows the structures and related components.

Table 6.4 ABC Architecture structures and components

Structure	Component
Business	***Business Processes*** All the banking business processes that are related to the aims and objectives ***Business Process Management*** All the business process management activities that are performed within the bank ***IT Control model*** All the governing activities that assist in the development and evolution of IT ***Bank Website Administration*** All the controlling activities that performed to monitor and maintain the website of the bank

Structure	Component
Technology	***Infrastructure*** All the hardware elements that is necessary for connecting users and computers i.e. transmission media, routers, repeaters etc. ***Tools and technologies*** The bank has various tool-sets such as XML, DIGIPASS, VACMAN, SOAP, UML, Java tools, SQL etc. ***Architecture*** The ABC bank has different sub-architectures such as data management, applications and security sub-architectures

As we noted that the enterprise architecture of the ABC bank consists of the technologies that are integrated with the business processes in order to meet the bank's mission and objectives. The architecture depicts that developers are instructed for the use of component models and service oriented development.

We can see that table 6.4 shows the structures and components of the architecture that may help in maintaining the alignment between business and IT. The business components of the architecture are very important to the architecture. We noted that the ABC bank has the process of analyzing the investment and for this purpose business drivers and the needs have been integrated. This analysis is important for the improvement of the systems efficiency and effectiveness provided the IT investment has also been taken into consideration.

We found in the study that the executives of the ABC bank strive to disseminate business information to the staff and other stakeholders in order to keep them abreast with the bank policies, rules and regulations, new services and products. All agreed that sharing information, planning for the upcoming events and supporting each other in the organization reduce the gap between business and IT as all staff would be aware of business processes and required technologies. A senior executive said that the alignment mechanism in the bank is in place where senior business executives and strategic management groups plan business and strategic planning along with the IT control. We observed that there are two mechanisms in the bank that exhibit the alignment between business and IT. The first mechanism is responsible for communication about business planning at all levels and full management support. The second mechanism is the intellectual that is responsible for monitoring and reviewing enterprise architecture in both business and IT domains, groups of executives and staffs.

Businesses are changing and hence a perfect synchronization between mechanisms cannot be achieved, in turn alignment is different in different times. Table 6.5 shows the mechanisms for alignment in the bank

Table 6.5 Mechanism for alignment in the bank

Communication mechanisms	Disseminating information of business planning Support from the highest management
Intellectual mechanisms	Auditing enterprise architecture both business and IT Top management forums Planning for strategy

We noted that the gap between business and IT cannot be reduced just only at high level mechanisms, but it is also necessary that low-level mechanisms be given consideration such as business training to the staff or training in new business processes and information technologies. We found the architecture of the bank intended to bridge the gap between business and IT and there were links between main business processes and IT components that were shown in the enterprise architecture.

We also conducted interviews within ABC bank with many executives, senior officials, manager, middle managers and supervisors of their respective department. We delivered 118 questionnaires to the people whom either we could not meet at all or partial interviews were conducted. We received 71 completed questionnaire and following checking and reliability test we selected 65 questionnaires for the required data [the data may be provided on request].

Following we show data in different tables that we received from different respondents in the bank to closed-ended questions (either in interviews or survey instruments). The questions were aiming at knowing the overall performance of the ABC bank. As we stated earlier, we used the Likert's scale with numerical values ranging from 1 to 5 where 1 represents 'Strongly Disagree' (SDA), 2 is used for 'Disagree' (DA), 3 is for 'Neutral' (N), 4 represents 'Agree' (A) and 5 is for 'Strongly Agree' (SA).

The table 6.6 shows the total numbers of responses in each item for organizational performance.

Table 6.6 Organizational Performance Items Responses

Item	Description	No. of Responses				
		5	4	3	2	1
FPS	Organization increased financial products and services	36	16	3	5	5
ASG	Annual sales growth is remarkable	34	18	3	5	5
CS	Level of customer satisfaction increased	32	22	3	4	4
OC	The operational cost has decreased	37	16	2	6	4
MS	The IT has facilitated to gain market share	27	26	2	6	4
RS	The staff are rewarded based on performance	32	14	4	9	6
OI	Overall image of our institution is increased	23	29	3	6	4
QPS	Quality of financial products and services has increased	30	24	2	5	4
ROI	The organization has excellent return on investment	37	18	1	6	3
IRR	New product or service has good internal rate of return	34	22	2	5	2

The table 6.7 shows the list of items in order of the scores on scale 1-5 that each item received in organizational performance.

Table 6.7 Organizational Performance Items Score

Item	Description	Score
IRR	Internal rate of return is good	4.24
ROI	Return on investment is excellent	4.23
CS	Customer satisfaction is increased	4.13
FPS	Financial products and services increased	4.12
OC	Operational cost decreased	4.10
QPS	Quality of products and services increased	4.09
ASG	Annual sales growth remarkable	4.09
MS	Market share gained due to IT	4.01
OI	Organization image improved	3.93
RS	Staff rewarded based on performance	3.87

Any business organization is a set of activities that include business model, strategy and operations. By business model we mean that how organization create and deliver values, strategy meets the aims and objectives of the organization and operations implement strategy that that comprised of people, processes and IT elements. The data in table 6.5 and 6.6 show the bank performance is good and the business model is working appropriately. It is important to note that in overall performance of the bank people did not strongly agree that IT has helped to gain market share. This is the only one parameter where people have shown a little different opinion. The scores in other items such as the quality of products and services is increased (QPS) and in turn the level of customers' satisfaction increased (CS) show that business processes are supported by the underlying IT, then why people have different opinion that IT did not help to gain market share. We will strive to find the answer in the following data tables. Although, the bank provides good services to the customers, we noted the bank does not provide frequent bonuses or rewards to employees (RS) based on their performance and this may have been one of the reasons that the image is not that glaring (OI).

The table 6.8 shows the measures for business strategies and the responses received from the respondents.

Table 6.8 Business Strategies Items Responses

Item	Description	No. of Responses				
		5	4	3	2	1
BSIT	The IT has significance in business strategies	12	7	4	22	20
BSP	IT people should be engaged in business strategies	11	10	6	23	15
BRIT	The IT role in business is to support business processes	36	10	4	8	7
BOGT	Organization is growing due to IT	28	20	5	8	4

Item	Description	No. of Responses				
		5	4	3	2	1
BMIT	Business managers should consult IT	37	12	5	6	5
BPRO	Business process reengineering should continue	36	16	3	7	3
BPAS	Personnel well aware of business and IT strategies	23	13	4	9	6
BART	Business architecture updated regularly	35	15	6	7	2
BSPC	Services and products introduced for competition	33	18	3	7	4
BOR	Organization is willing to take risk	16	12	3	22	12

The table 6.9 shows the total scores received by each item in business strategies measures

Table 6.9 Business Strategies Items Score

Item	Description	Score
BPRO	Business process reengineering should continue	4.15
BART	Business architecture updated regularly	4.13
BSPC	Services and products introduced for competition	4.09
BMIT	Business managers should consult IT	4.07
BRIT	IT role in business is just to support business	3.92
BOGT	Organization growing due to IT	3.92
BPAS	Personnel well aware of business & IT strategies	3.89
BOR	Organization willing to take risk	2.96
BSP	IT people should be engaged in business strategies	2.67
BSIT	IT has significance in business strategies	2.52

As business strategy is composed of corporate strategy, business and operation strategy, we see in tables 6.7 and 6.8 most of the people do not agree that IT has significance in business strategies and IT people should be engaged in business strategy (see items BSIT and BSP). This implies that operational levels between business and IT do not co-evolve. Since IT planners are not engaged in business strategies due to the lack of communication successful links between business objectives, IT strategy and underlying architecture insufficiently developed and a gap is created. The data shows that three levels are not co- evolving as shown in our co-evolutionary framework. Business people perceive the IT services are just to support the business processes and they do not consider the significance of IT personnel in business strategies. Our argument is supported by the data from BRIT that shows people consider IT as a tool to support business processes. Most of people are not well aware of business and IT strategies as shown in item BPAS. For a successful business it is important that business and IT environment are linked together. This requires the co-evolution throughout the three levels as the data depicts co-evolution does not occur in the bank throughout the first level (i.e. individual level) as we have shown in our framework. This validates our framework that co-evolution can occur at all three levels rather at any specific level. Albeit, the bank is performing well, but the performance can be improved by implementing our co-evolutionary framework as it enables IT people to develop a system that could reflect organization's needs and achieve business-IT alignment.

The organization needs to utilize the full capabilities of its IT infrastructure that is composed of technical (such as software, hardware, networks etc.) and human components (such as technical skills, capabilities and IT knowledge). As most of the people strongly agree that business processes should be reengineered continuously (item BPRO), it is important that all people should be well aware of it and this can be affective if all three levels co-evolve shown in our framework.

The table 6.10 shows the data for IT strategies measures and responses received from the bank staff.

Table 6.10 IT Strategies Items

Item	Description	No. of Responses				
		5	4	3	2	1
TICS	The IT investment linked with corporate strategy	17	16	5	12	15
TAT	The organization acquires new technology	22	13	4	15	11
TBA	The IT budget is considered as an expense	32	20	5	6	2
TLB	The lack of business knowledge in IT people	28	13	4	12	8
TUR	Information systems are updated with new IT	30	15	4	11	5

The table 6.11 shows the total scores in each item of the IT strategies items

Table 6.11 IT Strategies Items Scores

Item	Description	Score
TBA	IT budget is considered as expense	4.13
TUR	Information systems updated with new IT	3.83
TLB	Lack of business knowledge in IT people	3.63
TA	Organizations acquires new technology	3.30
TICS	IT investment linked with corporate strategy	3.12

Co-evolution in organization may not occur unless the evolving business processes are supported by the evolving technologies. As we see in tables 6.9 and 6.10 that most of the respondents consider IT budget as an expense (item TBA) that is the organization does not value the adaptation of technologies. This argument is supported by the data TUR and TA as well where new technologies are not readily acquired and updated with the new systems. The data shows the information systems in the bank are updated with the existing technologies due to financial restrictions. This also depicts that co-evolution does not occur effectively as when business and IT strategies are changed the lower levels do not co-evolve due to budget constraints and therefore, a misalignment occurs. This also validates the co-evolutionary framework that requires co-evolution from first level to the third level.

The case of the ABC bank illustrates that there is development in business as a result of business evolution (new services and products), but due to absence of evolving IT there is a gap between business and IT. Co-evolution in the bank may occur in result of a change that requires changes in all levels and components. Currently co-evolution does not occur since the architecture of the ABC bank does not co-evolve i.e. when the new services or products are introduced or new business strategies are adopted, the supporting technologies do not co-evolve. Secondly, the absence of appropriate communication between business and IT people at all levels causes the misalignment and does not allow co-evolving the system and the gap between the two entities arises.

Our co-evolutionary framework that is comprised of three levels will help to overcome such problems in an integrated fashion. When business or IT strategies are changed at strategic level, the operational level will support with the required technologies by looking into the required components and co- evolve the system and the IT infrastructure will fulfill the individual's requirements. Since each level in the framework interacts with another level co- evolution occurs at different levels.

6.3 Summary

The main aim of the chapter was to evaluate and validate the co-evolutionary framework in a financial institution. To achieve this, a case study was carried out in a financial institution and data was collected by using different research methods such as interviews, observations and questionnaire. A survey instrument was also designed for the purpose of collection of data from different employees in the organization. It was found that the co-evolution in the organization does not occur at all levels and impact of the co-evolution at strategic level does not propagate at all levels. Our findings in the case study show there is a gap between business and IT people and lack of communication from top level to lowest level causes the gap. The data also supports the argument that business strategies are developed without consulting IT personnel and therefore a misalignment occurs at the top. Consequently the operational and individual levels are affected and co-evolution does not take place effectively. The framework was found to be more efficient as it co-evolves all three levels in organization that may speed up the business processes.

7

Conclusion and Future Work

This chapter presents the summary of the book and the contribution to the knowledge by describing the answers of the research question. It also highlights limitation of the study and the directions for future work.

7.1 Summary

The purpose of this research study was to develop a co-evolutionary framework by integrating three levels i.e. strategic level, operational level and individual level. The study started with an extensive review of literature in order to find out relevant models. Some computational models were reviewed in order to provide a background of the proposed co-evolutionary framework that may be implemented in such contexts. A definition of computational model has been provided that is necessary to describe the behaviour of a system in terms of its components. Various alignment models and frameworks of business and IT were reviewed and almost all of them found to be conceptual and do not provide data. Since the research study aimed to be empirical therefore, there was a need to have enough knowledge about the factors and elements that are required to determine the co-evolution in organization. The reviewed literature helped to understand such factors and different levels of business and IT in organizations. The study carried out based on co-evolutionary methodology that expanded the knowledge of co-evolution of different entities. A co-evolutionary approach helps to determine the co-evolutionary dynamics between the entities in order to improve effectiveness of both the entities. In the research work a case study approach has also been used that supports an empirical investigation to be conducted for observing a real life phenomenon using several sources of information.

As a result of extensive literature review and in-depth study of co- evolution theory a co-evolutionary framework was developed. The proposed framework includes three levels of business and IT with their respective components (such as strategies, policies, rules, software, hardware, communication and network devices etc.). The three levels have been integrated by a k-mediator that facilitates co-evolution between levels of each entity. The benefit of the framework is that it ensures the co-evolution occurs at all three levels of business and IT. Therefore, business processes will become more efficient and effective in order to fulfill clients' requirements and more revenue generated.

The framework was evaluated and validated in a financial institution where a knowledgeable person in both the domains (i.e. business and IT) was considered as a k-mediator. The findings show that the co-evolution does not occur at all levels and the data obtained from different measurements exhibit good validation of the framework.

7.2 CONTRIBUTION

In order to highlight the main contribution of this book, we evaluate our work by giving the answer of the research question posed in the beginning of this book as:

Is there any systematic and scientific theory for co-evolution that may assist in discovering an efficient technique or method to reducing the gap between business and information technology?

The question has been answered in general by investigating the scientific theory for co-evolution that is based on biology and described by Ehrlich *et. al.*, [40] that when different species interact with each other in their environment the interaction causes evolutionary changes. This shows that each entity in co-evolutionary relationship influences each other and helps one another's evolution. This theory has helped us to relate business and IT in an integrated manner in an organizational environment. Almost all of the co-evolutionary models and frameworks presented by different researchers and practitioners are conceptual that stress on aligning business strategies and IT strategies.

None of the frameworks has investigated a scientific theory for co- evolution in an integrated fashion where three levels of business and IT have been studied using k-mediator. The proposed co-evolutionary framework is an empirical one that consists of three levels in organization i.e. strategic, operational and individual. The framework has used a knowledge mediator that provides the knowledge base to the framework. The three levels in organization facilitate co-evolution in organization. The proposed framework will help to understand co-evolution in business-IT environment and will aid organizations to expedite business processes that may generate more revenue. The framework has been validated in a financial institution where three levels were studied and co-evolution studied. The case study in a bank has provided data sufficient to evaluate and validate the framework.

As the research question was based on two sub-questions the first sub-question described as:

Does an integrated environment in an organization impact on the gap between business and IT ?

For a successful business it is important that all parts of an organization work strategically and operationally in the same direction at all levels. It is important that both business strategy and IT strategy work together in order to have positive impact on the strategic environment at strategic level and business processes efficiently perform at operational level. If business strategy and IT strategy are moving in different directions then business failure is imminent. Since companies invest heavily in IT they would like to achieve the business objectives with the help of IT function.

The answer of the question was found in the case study in the financial domain where data of different parameters showed that business and IT strategies affect the gap between business and IT. In tables 6.7 and 6.8 the BSIT and BSP data show that business and IT strategies do not co-evolve as most of the respondents in the bank do not agree that business IT personnel should be engaged in business strategies. This is the first level in organization and if the co- evolution does not take place at this level the lower levels may not co-evolve effectively. This validates our framework that co-evolution at all levels is necessary. Similarly, the BPAS data shows the personnel of the bank need to aware of business and IT strategies at individual level.

Similarly, in table 6.9 and 6.10 the data TBA shows that IT budget is restricted and considered as an expense and even the information systems are updated in result of any new requirement (see TUR data), it appears the change is updated with the existing technology that is the operational level does not co-evolve. The data TLB depicts that IT people have a lack of business knowledge and therefore they may not understand the business requirements properly. This shows the co-evolution does not take place at individual level.

We conclude that an integrated environment in organization does impact the gap between business and IT and this depends on organization how they co-evolve at different levels.

Another sub-question of the main research question stated as:

Is the linkage between business and information technology effective?

In business organizations IT influences the structure of the organizations. IT makes information readily available throughout the organization for decision making at different levels even centralized decision making at higher level. Therefore, organizations are adopting IT for not only expediting the business processes but also for making strategic decisions. The linkage between business and IT is very important and effective to maintaining the alignment between business and IT. When a change in business strategies occurs it must also change IT strategies as well [127]. This change may bring the co-evolution at lower levels i.e. operational and individual. If the business and IT are not linked together the co-evolution may not take place effectively.

The answer of the above sub-question is 'yes' as business and IT have an linkage. Further, the answer of the question was found in the case study in the financial domain where business processes are linked with the IT functions. The table 6.8 depicts the data where TUR and TBA show linkage between business and IT when the information systems are updated as soon as the business requirements are changed.

7.3 Future Work

This dissertation presents a co-evolutionary framework to reduce the gap between business and IT in an integrated fashion. For a successful co-evolution it is necessary that all three levels co-evolve with their respective components. The framework has been evaluated in a financial institution and cannot be generalized. In future, the framework can be validated in a large body of organizations or different type of business organizations. Since co-evolution is a continuous process and it occurs suddenly in result of a change, therefore, rate of evolution between both the entities is different. Researchers agree that the gap cannot be removed completely since both the entities evolve at different rates. Therefore, in future a theoretical framework can be built in order to determine the rate of evolution in each entity so that the co-evolution between business and IT could be controlled in desired manner.

References

Agarwal, R., and Sambamurthy, V., (2002). Principles and Models for Organizing the IT Function. MIS Quarterly Executive. March. http://misqe.org/V0101-02.pdf

Aier, S., and Winter, R., (2009), Virtual Decoupling for IT/Business Alignment –Conceptual Foundations, Architecture Design and Implementation Example, in: Business & Information Systems Engineering, 51(2), pp. 150-163

Alfawair, M., Aldabbas, O., Bartels, P., and Zedan, H., (2007), Grid Evolution, International Conference on Computer Engineering and Systems, ICCES'07, pp 158-163

Anderson, J., (2001), Information Technology Strategic Decision Making Approaches and Organizational Performance in different Industrial Settings, Journal of Strategic Information Systems, 10, pp. 101-119

Apostolopoulos, K., Pramataris, C., (1997), Information Technology Evaluation: Investments in Telecommunication Infrastructure, International Journal of Information Management, 21(4), pp. 287-296

Aprna, T., Bhawara, P., (2011), E-government Challenges and Cloud Benefits, In Proceedings of IEEE International Conference on Computer Science and Automation Engineering (CSAE), China, V4, pp. 351-354

Attewell, P., Rule, B., (1991), Survey and other Methodologies Applied to IT Impact Research: Experiences from a Comparative Study of Business Computing. In Kraemer, L., Cash, I., Nunamaker, F., vol. 3 chapter 10, Harvard Business School, Boston

Aversano, L., Bodhuin, T., and Tortorella, M., (2005), Assessment and Impact Analysis for Aligning Businesses Processes and Software Systems, SAC'05 ACM, NM

Benaroch, M., and Kauffman, J., (2000), Justifying Electronic Banking Network Expansion using Real Options Analysis, MIS Quarterly, 24, pp. 197-225

Benbya, H., and McKelvey, B., (2006), Using Coevolutionary and complexity theories to improve IS aligmnment: a multi-level approach, Journal of Information Technology, 21, 284-298

Bent F., (2011), Case Study, In Norman K. Denzin and Yvonna S. Lincoln, eds, The Sage Handbook of Qualitative Research, 4th ed, Chapter 17, pp. 301-316

Bergeron, F., Raymond, L., Rivard, S., (2001), Fit in Strategic Information Technology Management Research: An Empirical Comparison of Perspectives, The International Journal of Management Sciences, 29, pp. 125-142

Berkai, D., (2000), An Introduction to Peer-to-Peer Computing, Intel Corporation

Bevilacqua, M., Ciarapica, E., and Giacchetta, G., (2009), Business Process Reengineering of Supply Chain and Traceability System: A case study, Journal of Food Engineering, 93(1), pp. 13-22

Bidgoli, H., (2002), Electronic Commerce Principles and Practices, Academic Press, San Diego

Birol, B., (2005), Aligning IT with the Changes using the Goal-Driven Development for UML/MDA, Journal of Object Technology, 4(5), 49-65

Bob, H., and Mike, C., (2009), Software Project Management, 5th ed., McGraw Hill, UK

Brosilow, C., and Joseph, B., (2002), Techniques of Model-Based Control, Feedward Control, Chapter 9, Prentice Hall, New York

Burgelman, A., (1994), Fading memories: A process theory of strategic business exit in dynamic environments, Administrative Science Quarterly, 39(1), pp. 24-56

Carmines, E., Zeller, R., (1979), Reliability and Validity Assessment, SAGE Publications

Casati, F., Ilnicki, S., Jin, Li., Krishnamoorthy, V., and Shan, M., (2000), Adaptive and Dynamic Service Composition eFlow, International Conference on Information Systems Engineering (CAiSE), Stockholm, Sweden

Chan, E., Huff, L., Barclay, W., Copeland, G., (1997), Business Strategic Orientation, Information Systems Strategic Orientation and Strategic Alignment, Information Systems Research, 8(2), pp. 125-150

Chan, E., Sabherwal, R., Thatcher, B., (2006), Antecedents and Outcomes of Strategic IS Alignment: An Empirical Investigation, IEEE Transactions on Engineering Management, 51(3), pp. 27-47

Chan, S., (2000), Information Technology in Business Processes, Business Process Management Journal, 6(3), pp. 224-237

Charles, E., Rafael, L., and Ernst, F., (2008), The Co-evolution of Cultural Groups and Ingroup Favoritism, Science, 321(5897), pp. 1844-1849

Chau, K., and Lai, K., (2003), An Empirical Investigation of the Determinants of User Acceptance of Internet Banking, Journal of Organizational Computing and Electronic Commerce, 13(2), pp. 123-145

Chaudhry, A., and Rao, H.R., (1997), Introducing Client/Server Technologies in Information Systems Curricula, The Database for Advances in Information Systems, (28)(4)

Chuck, P., (2007). An Easy to Use Distributed Computing Network, In Proceedings of 38th SIGCSE Technical Symposium on Computer Science Education, USA, pp. 571-577

Clarke, A.M., (1998), The qualitative-quantitative debate: moving from positivism and confrontation to post-positivism and reconciliation, Journal of Advanced Nursing, 27(6), 1242-1249

Cook, D., Campbell, T., (1979), Quasi-Experimentation: Design and Analysis Issue for Field Settings, Houghton Mifflin Co, Boston

Cox, P., (1980), The Optimal Number of Response Alternatives for Scale: A Review, Journal of Marketing Research, 17(4), 407-422

Cragg, P., King, M., Hussin, H., (2002), IT Alignment and Firm Performance in Small Manufacturing Firms, Journal of Strategic Information Systems, 11, pp. 109-132

Cronbach, J., (1951), Coefficient alpha and the internal structure of tests, Psychometrika, 16, pp. 297-334

Cronford, T., and Smithson, S., (1997), Project Research in Information Systems: As Student's Guide. London: Macmillan Press

Croteau, M., and Bergeron, F., (2001), An Information Technology trilogy:Business strategy, technological deployment and organizational performance, Journal of Strategic Information Systems, 10(2), 77-99

Curtis, B., Kellner, I., and Over, J., (1992), Process Modeling, Communications of the ACM, 35(9), 75-90

Curtis, B., Kellner, I., and Over, J., (1992), Process Modeling, Communications of the ACM, 35(9), 75-90

Curtis, B., Kellner, M.I., and Over, J., (1992), ProcessModeling, Communications of the ACM, 35, 75-90

Daniel, G., Francisco, V., and Henri, C., (2009), Characterization Fault Tolerance in Genetic Programming, In Proceedings of Workshop on Bio- inspired Algorithms for Distributed Systems, Spain

Dansereau, F., Alutto, A., Yammarino, J., (1984), Theory Testing in Organizational Behavior: The Variant Approach, Prentice Hall, Englewood Cliffs, NJ

Danziger, N., and Kraemer, L., (1991), Survey Research and Multiple Operationism: The URBIS project methodology, In Kraemer, L., Cash, I., Nunamaker, F., vol. 3 chapter 13, Harvard Business School, Boston

David, C., (2010), E-business and E-commerce Management: strategy, implementation and practices, pp 560-590, Prentice Hall

Dillman, A., (1978), Mail and Telephone Surveys: The Total Design Method, Wiley, New York

Donald, R., (2001). Making the Software Business Case: Improving by the Numbers, Addison Wesely, Reading, Massachusetts

Dos Santos, L., Peffers, K., (1995), Rewards to Investors in Innovative Information Technology Applications: First Movers and Early Followers in ATMs, Organization Science, 6(3), pp. 241-259

Dos Santos, L., Peffers, K., Mauer, C., (1993), The Impact of Information Technology Investment Announcements on the Market Value of the Firm, Information Systems Research, 4(1), pp. 1-23

Ehrlich, D.R., and Raven, R.H., (1964), Butterflies and plants: a study in co-evolution, Evolution 18, 568-608

Emory, W., and Cooper, R., (1991), Business Research Methods (4th ed.), Irwin Publishing, Homewood, IL

Erdos, L., (1970), Professional Mail Surveys, McGraw Hills, New York, USA

Farbey, B., Land, F., and Target, T., (1994), A taxonomy of information systems applications: the benefits' evaluation ladder, European Journal Information Systems, 4, pp. 41-50

Feinstein, W. P., and Hawker, J.S., (2000), A Study of Technologies for Client/ Server Application, ACM 2000

Giaglis, G.M., Paul, R.J. and Doukidis, G.I., (1996), Simulation for Intra and Intra-organizational Business Process Modeling,Presented at Winter Simulation Conference, Coronado, CA

Greenwood, R., Balasubramaniam, D., Cimpan, S., Kirby, G., Micken, K., Morrison, R., Oquendo, F., Robertson, I., Seet, W., Snowdown, B., Wardboys, B., Zirintsis, E., (2003), Process Support for Evolving Architectures, Lecture Notes on Computer Science, 2786/2003, pp. 112-127, Springer

Gunasekaran, A., Love, Peter, D., Rahimi, F., Miele, R., (2001), A Model for Investment Justification in Information Technology Projects, International Journal of Information Management, 21, 349-364

Haes, S., and Grembergen, W., (2009), Exploring the Relationship between IT Governance Practices and Business/IT alignment through Extrteme Case Analysis in Belgian mid-to-large Size Financial Enterprises, Journal of Enterprise Information Management, 22(5), pp. 615-637

Hammer, M. and Champy, J., (1993), Re-engineering the Corporation; A Manifesto for Business Revolution, Harper Business, New York

Hammer, M., and Champy, J., (1993). Reengineering the Corporation: a Manifesto for Business Revolution, NY: HarperCollins

Hedman, J., and Kalling, T., (2003), The Business Model Concept: Theoretical Underpinning and Empirical Illustrations, European Journal of Information Systems, 12, 49-59

Heineman, G., and Council, W., (2001), Components-Based Software Engineering: Putting the Pieces Together, Addison Wesely

Henderson, C., and Venkatraman, N., (1999), Strategic Alignment: Leveraging information technology for transforming organizations IBM Systems Journal, 38, 472-484

Henderson, J., and Venkatraman, N., (1993), Strategic Alignment: Analysis of Information Technology for Transforming Organizations`, IBM Systems Journal, 32(1), pp. 472-484

Homann, H., Rill, M., and Wimmer, A., (2004), Flexible Value Structures in Banking, Communications of the ACM, 47(5), pp. 34-36

Hughes, J., (1994), The Philosophy of Social Research, Essex, Longman

Jacobson, I., Ericsson, M., and Jacobson, A., (1995), The Object Advantage: Business Process Reengineering with Object Technology, ACM Press, Addison-Wesley

Jan, S., Ulrik, F., Robert, L., Mathias, E., (2010), Enterprise Architecture Meta Models for IT/Business Alignment Situations, In Proceedings of 14th International Enterprise Distributed Object Computing Conference, Brazil, pp. 14-23

Justin, S., (2009), Co-evolution of Human and Machine, Neuroprosthesis in 21st Century, In Proceedings of IEEE Conference on the History of Technical Societies, pp. 1-4, PA, USA

Kalakota, R., and Whinston, B., (1996), Frontiers of Electronic Commerce, Reading, Massachusetts, Addison-Wesley

Kamath, S., (2011). Capabilities and Future: Linking Business and Application Architecture – I, In Proceedings of International Conference on Information Science and Applications (ICISA), Korea, pp. 1-7

Kauffman, S., (1993), The Origins of Order: Self-organization and selection in Evolution, Oxford University Press

Kauffman, S., (1995), At Home in the Universe, Penguin, England

Kecheng, L., and Keith, B., (2002), Co-Design of Business and IT Systems – Introduction by Guest Editors, Information Systems Frontiers, 4(3), pp. 251-256

Kerlinger, N., (1986), Foundation of Behavioral Research (3rd ed.), Rinehart and Winston Inc., New York

Khan, M.A., and Zedan, H., (2010), Alignment Strategies and Frameworks in Co-Evolution of Business and Information Technology, In Proceedings of IEEE International Conference on Information, Networking and Automation (ICINA), China, V1, pp 133-137

Khan, MA., and Zedan, H., (2011), Requirements for Co-evolution of Business and Information Technology, In Proceedings of IEEE International

Conference on Information Systems and Computational Intelligence (ICISCI2011), China, V1, pp 14-17

Kirby, C., Connor, H., Cutts, I., Dearle, A., Farkas, M., Morrison, R., (1992), Persistent Hyper Program, In: Albano, A., Morrison, R. (eds.) Proc. 5th International Conference on Peristent Object Systems, Italy, In Persistent Object Systems, pp. 86-106

Kling, R., (1996), Computerization and Controversy: Value Conflicts and Social Choices, Academic Press, San Diego

Koza, M.P. and Lewin, A., (1998), The Co-evolution of Strategic alliances, Organization Science, No. 9, 255-264

Kraemer, K., (1991), The Information Systems Research Challenge: Survey Research Methods, Introduction. In Kraemer, L., Cash, I., Nunamaker, F., 3, Harvard Business School, Boston

Kruchten, P., Obink, J., and Stafford, J., (2006), The Past, Present and Future for Software Architecture, IEEE Software, 23(2), pp. 22-30

Kung-Kiu, L., and Zheng, W., (2007), Software Component Models, IEEE Transaction on Software Engineering, 33(10), pp. 70-724

Lau, K, Ukis, V., Velasco, P., and Wang, Z., (2006), A Component Model for Separation of Control Flow from Computation in Component-Based Systems, Electronic Notes in Theoretical Science, 163, pp 57-69

Lau, K., and Wang, Z., (2005), A Taxonomy of Software Component Models, Proceedings of Conference on Software Engineering and Advanced Applications, EUROMICRO

Lewin, Y., and Volberda, W., (1999), Prolegomena on Co-evolution: A Framework for Research on Strategy and New Organizational Forms, Organization Science, vol. 10, no. 5, pp. 519-534

Maes, R., (1999), Reconsidering Information Management through a Generic Framework, Primavera Working Paper 99-03 [http://primavera.fee.uva.nl]

Maes, R., Rijsenbrij, D., Truijens, O., Goedvolk, H., (2000), Redefining Business-IT Alignment through a Unified Framework, Primavera Working Paper 2000-19 [http://primavera.fee.uva.nl]

Mangione, W., (1995), Mail Surveys: Improving the Quality, Thousand Oaks, Sage Publications, CA

Marcus, V., Dieter, H., and Kieth H., (2011), Strategic ICT Alignment in Uncertain Environments: An Empirical Study in Emergency Management Organizations, In Proceedings of 44th Hawaii International Conference on System Sciences, pp. 1-9, Hawaii, USA

Martin, J., Jens, W., and Werner, E., (2010), A Model-Driven Framework for Business IT Alignment, Int. J. Internet and Enterprise Management, 6(3), pp. 233 – 247

McKelvey, B., (1999), Avoiding complexity catastrophe in coevolutionary pockets: strategies for rugged landscapes. Organization Science, 10(3): 294-321

Mckelvey, B., (1999). Self-organization, complexity, catastroph, and microstate models at the edge of chaos, In Baun JAC and Mchelvey, B. (eds), Variations in organization science, In honor of Donald T. Campbell, Thousand Oaks, CA, Sage, 279-307

Mckelvey, B., (1999). Visioning Leadership vs Distributed Intelligence: Strategy, Microcoevolution, Complexity, In proceedings of EIASM Workshop, Brussels

McKelvey, B., (2002), Managing Coevolutionary Dynamics: Some leverage points, 18th EGOS Conference, Barcelona, Spain

Meng. J., Sue, S., Lam, H., and Helal, A., (2002), Achieving dynamic inter-organizational workflow management by integrating business processes, events and rules, Hawaii International Conference on System Sciences, USA

Michael, P., (2002), Microsoft Architecture Overview, .Network Center, Microsoft Corporation [www.msdn.microsoft.com]

Mingfang, L., and Ye, R., (1999), Information Technology and Firm Performance: Linking with Environmental Strategic and Managerial Contexts, Information and Management, 33, pp. 43-51

Mingfang, L., Ye, R., (1999), Information Technology and Firm Performance: Linking with Environmental Strategic and Managerial Contexts, Information & Management, 33, pp. 43-51

Mitelton-Kelly, E., and Papaefthimiou, M., (2000), Coevolution and an Enabling Infrastructure: A Solution to Legacy, Systems Engineering for Business Process Change, Springer-Verlag, 1st ed.

Mitelton-Kelly, E., and Papaefthimiou, M., (2000), Coevolution and an Enabling Infrastructure: A Solution to Legacy, Systems Engineering for Business Process Change, Springer-Verlag, 1st ed.

Mitelton-Kelly, E., and Papaefthimiou, M., (2000), Co-evolution of Diverse Elements Interacting within a Social Ecosystem, System Engineering for Business Process Change, pp 253-273

Mitleton-Kelly, E., (2000), Complexity: Partial Support for BPR, System Engineering for Business Process Change, Chapter 3, edited by Henderson, P., Springer-Verlag

Mizan, A., Frank, G., (2011), An Automatic Trace Based Performance Evaluation Model Building for Parallel Distributed Systems, In Proceedings of Second Joint WOSP/SIPEW International Conference on Performance Engineering ICPE '11, Germany, pp. 61-72,

Morrison, R., Balasubramaniam, D., Kirby, G., Mickan, K., Wardboys, B., Greenwood, R., Robertson, I., and Snowdown, B., (2007), A framework for supporting dynamic systems co-evolution, Autom Softw Eng, 14, 261-292

Nunnaly, C., Bernstein, H., (1994), Psychometric Guide (2nd ed.), McGraw Hill, New York

Nunnaly, J., (1978), Psychometric Theory, McGraw Hill, New York

Olivia, D., and Arindam, D., (2008). Performability Evaluation of Mobile Client-Server Systems, SAC '08, Brazil, pp. 2197 - 2201

Oppenheim, A., (2005), Questionnaire Design, Interviewing and Attitude Measurement, Biddles Ltd, UK

Oquendo, F., Cimpan, S., Balasubramanim, D., Kirby, G., Morrison, R., (2002), The ArchWare ADL: Definition of the Textual Concrete Syntax, European RTD Project IST-2001-32360, Deliverable D 1.2b

Pajaro, J.R., (2004), A Peer-to-Peer Computing Communication Cost Model, Book, University of texas at El Paso

Papp, D., (2004), Assessing Strategic Alignment in Real Time, Journal of Informatics Education Research, vol. 6 no. 1

Parahoo, A. K., (1997), Nursing Research, Principles, Process and Issues, London, McMillan

Perrott, B., (2005). Towards a manager's model of e-business strategy decisions, Journal of General Management, vol. 30(4), pp.73-89

Premkumar, G., and Ramamurthy, K., (1995), Implementation of Electronic Data Interchange: An Innovation Diffusion Perspective, Journal of Information Systems, 11(2), 157-186

Preston, D., and Karahanna, E., (2009), How to Develop a Shared Vision: The Key to IS Strategic Alignment, MIS Quarterly Executive, 8(1), pp. 1-8

Proctor, S., (1998), Linking philosophy and method in the research process: The case of realism, Nurse Researcher, 5(4), 73-90

Pyzdek, T., (2003), The Six Sigma Handbook, McGraw Hill, New York

Rafael, M., and Jan, E., (2011), The Impact of Environmental Change on Host-parasite Co-evolutionary Dyanmics, In Proceedings of Royal Society B, 278, pp. 2283-2292

Rathnam, G., Justin, J., and Joseph H., (2005), Alignment of Business Strategy and IT Strategy: A case study of fortune 50 financial services company, Journal of Information Systems, 45(2)

Reich, H., and Benbasat, I., (2000), Factors that Influence the Social Dimension of Alignment between Business and Information Technology Objectives, Management Information Systems Quarterly, 24, pp. 81-113

Rolf-Dieter, K., and Jurgen, R., (1999), Do IT Smart: Seven Rules for Superior Information Technology Performance, The Free Press, a Division of Simon & Schuster, Inc., New York

Rosenberg, J., (1998), Teach Yourself CORBA in 14 days, SAMs Publishing

Ross, W., Weill, P., and Robertson, C., (2006), Enterprise Architecture as Strategy – Creating a Foundation for Business Execution, Harvard Business School Press, Boston, USA

Rosti, E., Serazzi, G., Smirni, S., and Squillante, M., (1998), The Impact of I/O on Program Behavior and Parallel Scheduling, Proc ACM SIGMETRICs '98 Conf. Measurement and Modeling of Computer Systems and Performance '98, pp 57-65

Sabherwal, R., and Chan, E., (2001), Alignment between business and ISstrategies: A study of prospectors, analyzers and defenders, Information Systems Research, 12(1)

Sabherwal, R., and Chan, Y., (2001), Alignment between Business and IS Strategies: A study of prospectors, analyzers and defenders, Information Systems Research 12(1) 11-33

Samarin, A., (2008). How to simplify the evolution of business process lifecycles, www.improving-bpm-systems.com

Scott, M.S., Smith, H.J., and Jane, C.L., (2005), The Power of Business Model, Business Horizon, 48, pp 199-207

Sinur, J., McCoy, D., and Thompson, J., (2003). Gartner Application Integration and Middleware Strategies, Research Note T-19-4751, The Gartner Group

Stake, R.E., (1994), In Handbook of Qualitative Research , edited by Denzin NK and Lincoln YS, Sage, London

Strnadl, F., (2006), Aligning Business and IT: The Process-Driven Architecture Model, Information Systems Management, 23(4), 67-77

Tallon, P., (2007), A Process-oriented Perspective on the Alignment of Information Technology and Business Strategy, Journal of Management Information Systems, 24(3), pp. 227-268

Tivnan, F., (2005), Coevolutionary Dynamics and Agent-Based Models in Organization Science, Proc. of 2005 Winter Simulation Conference, Kuhl eds

Val, H., Sid, H., Peter, T., (2010), The Impact of IS-Marketing Alignment on Marketing Performance and Business Performance, The Database for Advances in Information Systems, 41(1), pp. 36-55

Van Horn, L., (1973), Empirical Studies on Management Information Systems, Databases, 5, pp. 172-180

Venketraman, N., (1994), IT-Enabled Business Transformation: From Automation to Business Scope Redefinition, Sloan Management Review, 35(2), pp 73-87

Wardboys, C., Kawalek, P., Robertson, I., and Greenwood, M., (1999), Business Information Systems: A Process Approach, McGraw-Hill, NY

Weil, P., and Vitale, R., (2001), Place to Space, Migrating e-Business Models, Harvard School of Business, Boston, USA

Weske, M., (2007), Business Process Management Concepts, Languages, Architecture, 1st ed, Springer-Verlag Berlin Heidelberg

Winter, S., and Taylor, S., (1996), The Role of IT in the Transformation of Work: A Comparison of Post-Industrial and Proto-Industrial Organization, Information System Research, 7(1), pp, 5-21

Xiaochuan, W., (2004), A Co-evolution Approach to Sensor Placement and Control Design for Robot Obstacle Avoidance, In Proceedings of 2004 International Conference on Information Acquisition, pp. 107-112

Xueying, W., Xiongwei, Z., and Longbin, J., (2008), A Method of Business and IT Alignment Based on Enterprise Architecture, IEEE International Conference on Service Operations and Logistics, and Informatics, pp. 740-745

Yang, J., and Papazoglou, M., (2000), International Support for Electronic Business, Communications of the ACM, 43(6), pp. 45-46

Yin, R., (1984), Case Study Research: Design and Methods. Sage Publications, California, 11-15

Zedan, H, Zhou, S., Sampat, N., Chen, X., Cau, A., and Yang, H., (2001). K-Mediator: Towards Evolving Information Systems, IEEE International Conference on Software Maintenance (ICSM'01), pp 520-527

Zmud, W., (1982), Diffusion of Modern Software Practices: Influence of Centralization and Formalization, Management Science, 28(12), pp. 1421-1431

Appendices

Appendix

Following are the indicative questions that were used in semi-structured and unstructured case interviews and survey instrument

Please indicate [√] against each of your answer

Section I: Overall Organizational Performance

1. Our organization has increased the number of financial products and services within last year

   [ ] Strongly Agree

   [ ] Agree

   [ ] Neutral

   [ ] Disagree

   [ ] Strongly Disagree

2. Our annual sales growth position is remarkable as relative to our competitors

   [ ] Strongly Agree

   [ ] Agree

   [ ] Neutral

   [ ] Disagree

   [ ] Strongly Disagree

3. The level of customer satisfaction has increased as compare to the previous years

   [ ] Strongly Agree

   [ ] Agree

   [ ] Neutral

   [ ] Disagree

   [ ] Strongly Disagree

4. The operational cost within organization has decreased

   [ ] Strongly Agree

   [ ] Agree

[ ] Neutral

[ ] Disagree

[ ] Strongly Disagree

5. The IT has facilitated our organization to gain market share as compare to competitors

   [ ] Strongly Agree

   [ ] Agree

   [ ] Neutral

   [ ] Disagree

   [ ] Strongly Disagree

6. Our organization always rewards to staff based on the business performance

   [ ] Strongly Agree

   [ ] Agree

   [ ] Neutral

   [ ] Disagree

   [ ] Strongly Disagree

7. We understand the overall image of our organization has improved

   [ ] Strongly Agree

   [ ] Agree

   [ ] Neutral

   [ ] Disagree

   [ ] Strongly Disagree

8. The quality of our financial products and services has increased

   [ ] Strongly Agree

   [ ] Agree

   [ ] Neutral

   [ ] Disagree

   [ ] Strongly Disagree

9. We consider our organization has excellent return on investment

   [ ] Strongly Agree

   [ ] Agree

   [ ] Neutral

   [ ] Disagree

   [ ] Strongly Disagree

10. In our financial institution any new launch of product or service has a good internal rate of return

   [ ] Strongly Agree

[ ] Agree
[ ] Neutral
[ ] Disagree
[ ] Strongly Disagree

Section II: Business and IT Strategies

11. In our organization IT has a significant involvement in shaping our business strategy
    [ ] Strongly Agree
    [ ] Agree
    [ ] Neutral
    [ ] Disagree
    [ ] Strongly Disagree
12. We understand that IT people should be engaged in forming business strategy
    [ ] Strongly Agree
    [ ] Agree
    [ ] Neutral
    [ ] Disagree
    [ ] Strongly Disagree
13. In my opinion IT role in our organization is to support business processes
    [ ] Strongly Agree
    [ ] Agree
    [ ] Neutral
    [ ] Disagree
    [ ] Strongly Disagree
14. We think that our organization is growing due to implementation of technology
    [ ] Strongly Agree
    [ ] Agree
    [ ] Neutral
    [ ] Disagree
    [ ] Strongly Disagree
15. We are of the view that business managers should consult with the IT managers in preparing business strategy
    [ ] Strongly Agree
    [ ] Agree
    [ ] Neutral

[ ] Disagree

[ ] Strongly Disagree

16. We consider the business process reengineering should be a routine work within organization

    [ ] Strongly Agree

    [ ] Agree

    [ ] Neutral

    [ ] Disagree

    [ ] Strongly Disagree

17. Our organization regularly reviews and upgrades the business architecture in result of any IT innovation

    [ ] Strongly Agree

    [ ] Agree

    [ ] Neutral

    [ ] Disagree

    [ ] Strongly Disagree

18. Our financial organization offers new services and products to be a competitive in the industry

    [ ] Strongly Agree

    [ ] Agree

    [ ] Neutral

    [ ] Disagree

    [ ] Strongly Disagree

19. Our organization is always willing to take risks

    [ ] Strongly Agree

    [ ] Agree

    [ ] Neutral

    [ ] Disagree

    [ ] Strongly Disagree

20. The IT investment in our organization is linked with the corporate strategy

    [ ] Strongly Agree

    [ ] Agree

    [ ] Neutral

    [ ] Disagree

    [ ] Strongly Disagree

21. Our organization acquires state of the art technology (i.e. software, hardware) as soon as the need arises

    [ ] Strongly Agree

[ ] Agree
[ ] Neutral
[ ] Disagree
[ ] Strongly Disagree

22. In our firm IT budget is restricted and considered as an expense rather an asset

[ ] Strongly Agree
[ ] Agree
[ ] Neutral
[ ] Disagree
[ ] Strongly Disagree

23. Our IT people have difficulty in understanding business requirements due to the lack of business knowledge

[ ] Strongly Agree
[ ] Agree
[ ] Neutral
[ ] Disagree
[ ] Strongly Disagree

24. Our information systems are updated as soon as new business requirements are introduced

[ ] Strongly Agree
[ ] Agree
[ ] Neutral
[ ] Disagree
[ ] Strongly Disagree

25. We are well aware of our organization's business and IT strategies and objectives

[ ] Strongly Agree
[ ] Agree
[ ] Neutral
[ ] Disagree
[ ] Strongly Disagree

26. We believe that enterprise architecture can help reducing the gap between business and IT

[ ] Strongly Agree
[ ] Agree
[ ] Neutral

[ ] Disagree

[ ] Strongly Disagree

Section III: Architecture and Environment

27. Please describe the method that is used to develop architecture in your organization
28. In your organization what resources are used to implement the enterprise architecture
29. Please elaborate the parts that are functional and non-functional in the architecture in your organization
30. In your organization what are the inherited structures (e.g. business, applications, infrastructure) in the architecture
31. Please list down different components of your organizational IT environment (e.g. software, hardware, staff, modeling tools and languages)
32. Please describe any system development or project management method that is used for developing information system or executing a project in your organization
33. What business planning communications for business strategy and information systems planning activities are available in your organization
34. Please describe whether information systems in your organization deliver business strategies to help you
35. Please describe the recent business functions that have been reviewed and updated to fulfill customers requirements and supported technologies

Section IV: Respondent's Background

36. Gender

    [ ] Male

    [ ] Female

37. Age

    [ ] 20-30

    [ ] 30-40

    [ ] 40-50

    [ ] More than 50

38. Education

    [ ] High School [ ] Graduate

    [ ] Post Graduate

39. Current Position

    [ ] Executive/Management (CEO,VP)

    [ ] Middle Manager

[ ] Supervisor

40. Annual Income

    [ ] Less than $20,000

    [ ] $20,000 - $40,000

    [ ] $40,000 – $80,000

    [ ] More than $80,000

Thank you for your cooperation

Index